# CHARLIE TROTTER'S

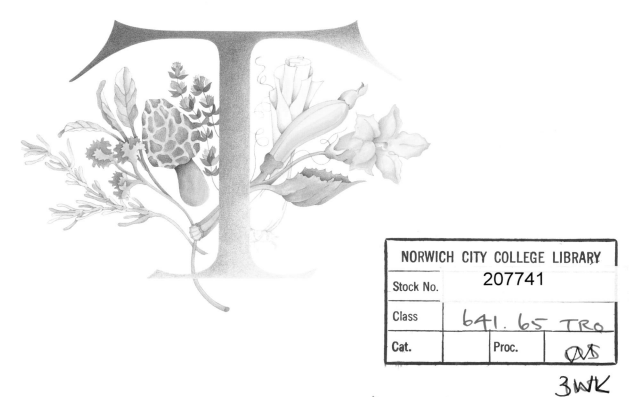

# VEGETABLES

*Recipes by*
Charlie Trotter

*Photography by*
Tim Turner

*Wine Notes by*
Joseph Spellman

Ten Speed Press, Berkeley, California

*Live in each season as it passes, breathe the air, drink the drink, taste the fruit and resign yourself to the influences of each.*

HENRY DAVID THOREAU

I would like to dedicate this book to my son, Dylan, who eats some vegetables, when coaxed; to my wife, Lynn, who eats vegetables when they are somehow paired with sushi; and to my mother Dona-Lee who eats just about anything I make.

CHARLIE TROTTER

# CONTENTS

# INTRODUCTION

*The near end of the street was rather dark and had mostly vegetable shops. Abundance of vegetables—piles of white and green fennel, like celery, and great sheaves of young purplish, sea-dust colored artichokes…long strings of dried figs, mountains of big oranges, scarlet large peppers, a large slice of pumpkin, a great mass of colours and vegetable freshness…*

D. H. LAWRENCE

I have always considered vegetable cookery the most interesting part of cuisine. Vegetables provide an incredible depth and complexity in both flavor and texture, not to mention an extraordinary range of colors and shapes, that cannot be matched by beef or salmon. Whereas meat and fish tend to be one-dimensional in their flavors and textures, vegetables provide a kaleidoscopic assortment of possibilities. At the restaurant, I invariably support the meat and fish dishes on the nonvegetable menu with significant vegetable components of two, three, or more items. I must confess though, I am far from a vegetarian. I just happen to be in love with the experience of touching, cooking, and eating the multitude of vegetables, fruits, legumes, and grains. It is sincerely one of the most sensual joys of my life.

The act of preparing vegetables is an especially life-giving exercise, primarily because it leads to serving and eating foods that are inherently good for you. But I do not think of vegetable cuisine in terms of health food, alternative food, or spa food, and, as a result, I do not create vegetable dishes based on nutritional values. I believe that such things fall into place naturally. If one pursues flavor first and foremost and works with extraordinarily fresh seasonal foodstuffs, possibly even organic foodstuffs, then one is surely going to eat healthfully. I prefer to get my good health as a by-product of eating wonderful, tasty, sensual foods, which nourish the soul and spirit as well as the body.

At the restaurant I work with a network of approximately fifty different farmers, growers, foragers, and other less conventional purveyors. For instance, I get amazing tiny lettuces and haricots verts from a small garden at Cabrini Green, a Chicago housing project, which is tended by teenagers and grade school kids. Essentially, I go out of my way to get the best fruits and vegetables possible. But today, more than ever, you can easily find great produce at your local market as well. Or you may even try your hand at growing your own produce. In the summer months my wife, Lynn, grows heirloom tomatoes, chiles, and fifteen different herbs in our backyard while our high-rise dwelling neighbors grow similar foods in container gardens on their balconies. To me, this is irrefutable evidence that Americans have come to value the full tastes, irregular shapes, and surprising textures of carefully tended fruits and vegetables. Besides, the desire to grow things seems almost innate. It is the ultimate reaffirmation of life.

Use this book as a guide; the recipes certainly do not have to be followed to the letter. You will discover that, with a little effort and care, it is not difficult to make truly remarkable food for your family and friends, and that sharing it always makes the effort worthwhile. And perhaps you will be pleasantly reminded why sharing the food experience is so important. Or, as Antonia Till put it, "…even those for whom cooking is an oppressive chore or source of self-doubting anxiety, acknowledge that a meal shared by friends and family is one of the bonding rituals without which the family, society even, can fall apart." ‍ It would benefit us all to eat more meals together. Nothing would satisfy me more than if this celebration of vegetables inspired you to do just that.

ROOK...? 
**TABLE GRAPES**
CAL-WESTERN FARMING COMPANY
VISALIA, CALIFORNIA 93292
PRODUCT OF U.S.A.

*Boy...*
A MARK OF EXCELLENCE

## Anthony's Red Flame Seedless Grapes
NET WT. 22 LBS.
Anthony Vineyards Inc., Bakersfield, CA 93309  PRODUCE OF U.S.A.
**TABLE GRAPES**

KIRSCHENMAN ENT...

PRODUCE OF U.S.A
NET WT. 22 LBS.

## NATIVE SON
HILLSIDE ACRES
QUALITY
TABLE GRAPES
COACHELLA, CA 92736

PRODUCE OF U.S.A.
SIZE 8
**BO...**
FRES...
Grown & Packed by: M &...

...T LADY
...LL MAT.    2 4 5    42

## ...ide OF THE Fields
...FORNIA FREESTONE PEACHES

PRODUCE
**Sa...**
GIRDLED
GROWERS  PACKERS

...LIENTE

# WINE NOTES

Wine, in its elevation from the earth to the stem, is the vital elixir of an exalted meal. This is as true of a simple garden luncheon as it is of a ten-course degustation, and as central to the success of the social milieu as the foodstuffs of the season that are shared at table. When enjoyed alone, rare, old, and expensive wines can certainly convey their own excellence, in a transparent sensual experience, but they only become complete when they are part of the consummation of a meal.

Thus the range of wines served at Charlie Trotter's not only demonstrates an affinity for creative, beautiful, and delicious food, it also exemplifies winemaking excellence. ❧ Each recipe in this book includes recommendations for wines that are appropriate with the flavors of the dish. In developing a wine-friendly cuisine with vegetables, fruits, and grains, these recommendations rely on flavor-component integration rather than a more typical approach of balancing fats and proteins with acids and tannins. These elements are generally lacking in vegetable preparations, and their absence makes the use of many red wines impossible. The types of wines we choose to feature in the isolated experience of tasting each dish are drawn from the pool of quality regions and producers that are long-time favorites of the restaurant, with occasional appearances from new discoveries or atypical styles. ❧ The recommendations are empirical, not theoretical; rarely do predicted wine styles seem to fit the final form of a dish. And vintage variation, availability, and seasonality are considerations that may alter the home chef's wine choices. More important, the total effect of a meal should be considered when wines are being chosen; specific circumstances (the formality of the meal, the intimacy level of the guests, even the size of the party, for example) inform wine decisions far more than the individual dishes or foodstuffs. Many wine preferences will change because of the sequencing of dishes and the positioning of a given course. And, of course, the scope of one's cellar and the kinds of wines one likes should be the paramount informant for building a successful meal with wine. ❧ These cautions are not intended to diminish the relevance of the wine recommendations. We hope they guide, not limit, your wine experience; they are intended to challenge rather than solve the questions that each dish presents, both to the chef's mind and the sommelier's. Many wines "work" with many foods, and the more refined the food the better the wines should be. And finding those magical moments of pleasure—when the wine and food create friction, dialogue, intrigue—and enjoying a greater experience than the individual flavor components would suggest, ennobles the human enterprise of good wine, good food, and good taste.

JOSEPH SPELLMAN, SOMMELIER, CHARLIE TROTTER'S

To me, each **January** day feels like the morning after a great party. The crescendo of holiday celebrations—and indulgences—fades and our coordinates in the cycle of seasons are never more apparent: winter is truly upon us! ☙ Now is the time to fortify and nourish the body and soul with hearty, simple food. The instinct to do so has as much to do with the weather outside as it does with the climate within. While the chilled earth offers up humble roots and tubers, the mind and palate crave simplicity. And so, January is the perfect time for potatoes in any form, salsify, cabbage, slow-braised endive, rices, carrots, turnips, collard greens, roasted vegetable stews, heady cheeses, and citrus fruits. Comfort food, like my Six-Onion Risotto, becomes sublime when savored before a roaring fire. These hearty foods are naturally juxtaposed with the austerity of January, when everyday vegetables taste especially delicious after you have shoveled the walk.

# Baby Carrot Terrine with Shiitake Mushroom Salad, Carrot Juice Reduction, Dill Oil, and 50-Year-Old Balsamic Vinegar

*A terrine of this sort is a wonderful way to present vegetables if you desire a particularly elegant preparation. Of course, you could simply toss the ingredients together as a salad and get the same flavor. This dish marries the striking flavors of a few ingredients: carrots, dill, yogurt, shiitake mushrooms, and aged balsamic vinegar. The combination comes across with marvelous clarity, yet no one flavor dominates. The addition of Japanese togarashi provides a pleasant jolt to the palate.*

**Serves 4 to 6**

*8 bunches baby Belgian carrots*
*1 tablespoon olive oil*
*Salt and pepper*
*4 cups carrot juice*
*4 sheets gelatin*
*3 sprigs fresh dill, chopped*
*1 cup roasted shiitake mushrooms*
*1 small bunch blanched Swiss chard*
*1 cup Pickling Juice (see Appendices)*
*1/2 cup Yogurt Sauce (recipe follows)*
*1/4 cup julienned English cucumber*
*Dill Oil (see Appendices)*
*50-year-old balsamic vinegar*
*Togarashi*

METHOD  Peel the baby carrots and cut off both ends. Toss with olive oil, season with salt and pepper, and roast at 350 degrees for 20 to 30 minutes, or until tender. In a small saucepan, simmer 3 cups of the carrot juice for about 45 minutes, or until you have about 3 tablespoons of carrot reduction. Strain through a fine-mesh sieve. In a small saucepan, bring the remaining cup of carrot juice to a simmer, then strain. Place the gelatin in 2 cups of lukewarm water, let sit 2 minutes, then drain and squeeze out the excess water. Place the gelatin sheets in the hot carrot juice and allow to dissolve completely. This is your carrot aspic. Reserve 2 to 3 tablespoons of the aspic for later use. Chop 2 sprigs of dill and set aside.

Assemble the terrine by lining the mold (an 8 by 1½ by 2¼-inch terrine mold is best, but other similar-size molds will also work) with a piece of plastic wrap large enough to hang over the edges of the mold. Dip the roasted carrots in the carrot aspic and lay them side by side in the lined terrine mold, forming the first layer; make sure that there are no gaps or holes. After you have completed the first layer of the terrine, season with salt and pepper. Continue the process, pressing firmly after each layer to ensure a solid structure. When you are halfway up the mold, sprinkle on half of the dill. Dip three-quarters of the roasted shiitake mushrooms in the aspic and lay over the layer of dill. Top with a final layer of dill, reserving about 1 teaspoon for garnish. Continue with 2 or 3 more layers of roasted carrots until you reach the top of the terrine mold. Cover with the overhanging plastic wrap and refrigerate for 3 hours, or until firm.

To make the wrap, blanch the Swiss chard in boiling salted water and shock in ice water. Carefully remove the whole leaves and remove the inner core with a knife. Blot on a paper towel and lay flat on a piece of plastic wrap, creating a single layer of Swiss chard the length and circumference of the terrine. Brush with a light coat of carrot aspic. Carefully unwrap the chilled terrine and invert it onto the bottom edge of the Swiss chard. Wrap the Swiss chard around the terrine, then wrap the whole terrine with the plastic wrap to help keep its form. Refrigerate until needed.

Let the remaining shiitake mushrooms steep in the Pickling Juice for 1 hour, then julienne and toss with 1 tablespoon of the Yogurt Sauce. Toss the cucumber with 1 tablespoon of Yogurt Sauce and season to taste with salt and pepper. Remove the terrine from the mold and cut in ½-inch-thick slices with the plastic wrap on (remove the plastic wrap before serving).

ASSEMBLY  Place a slice of the terrine in the center of each plate. At the top and bottom of the terrine, place a small mound of cucumber salad. At the sides of the terrine, place a small mound of pickled shiitake mushrooms. Drizzle the Yogurt Sauce around the terrine along with the Dill Oil, balsamic vinegar, and the carrot reduction. Place some fresh dill around the terrine and top with a sprinkle of togarashi.

## Yogurt Sauce

Yield: about 10 tablespoons

*1/2 cup plain yogurt*
*2 tablespoons rice vinegar*
*2 teaspoons minced gingerroot*
*1 jalapeño, seeded, stem removed, and minced*
*Salt and pepper*

METHOD  Combine the ingredients in a small bowl and season with salt and pepper. Whisk until smooth.

## Wine Notes

This attractive dish includes many bursts of contrasting textures and flavors. Initial tastings proved that wines of fairly high acidity, like a Premier Cru Chablis from Dauvissat and a halbtrocken Riesling from Selbach-Oster, allowed all these flavors to comingle. Another tasting, in which the spicy elements were more prominent, showed a lean Albarino from Morgadio to support the dish. Oaky wines are to be avoided.

# Six-Onion Risotto with
# Red Wine—Black Olive Sauce

*Onions and black olives—it's hard to find a better combination. This dish is my version
of comfort food, satisfying and rich with sweetness from the onion and just the right salty edge
from the olives. The risotto could be served before the main course or as an entrée by simply
increasing the portion. Meat eaters might enjoy sliced chicken breast fanned on top of the risotto.*

**Serves 4**

*8 red cipolline onions, peeled*

*8 yellow cipolline onions, peeled*

*8 purple pearl onions, peeled*

*4 tablespoons butter*

*1/2 cup pitted Greek black olives*

*3 cups Burgundy*

*Salt and pepper*

*3 shallots, thinly sliced*

*2 tablespoons flour*

*2 cups grapeseed oil*

*10 baby leeks, cleaned*

*1/2 cup diced Spanish onion*

*2 cloves garlic, minced*

*1 cup arborio rice*

*4 cups hot water or Chicken Stock
(see Appendices)*

*1/4 cup Parsley Juice (see Appendices)*

METHOD  Place the cipolline and pearl onions on a sheet pan with 1 tablespoon of the butter. Roast in the oven at 350 degrees for 15 to 20 minutes, turning occasionally, until they are golden brown. Remove from oven and cut into quarters. Coarsely chop 1 tablespoon of olives and reserve for garnish. Place the Burgundy in a small saucepan and simmer over medium heat for about 40 minutes, or until reduced to 2/3 cup. Purée the Burgundy reduction with the remaining black olives in a blender on medium. Strain through a fine-mesh sieve and season to taste with salt and pepper.

Toss the shallots with the flour. Lightly dust off the excess flour and fry in the grapeseed oil until golden brown. Remove from the oil, blot on paper towels, and season to taste with salt and pepper.

Blanch the leeks in boiling salted water for 2 to 3 minutes, or until tender. Immediately shock in ice water.

Cut the leeks on the bias into 1/4-inch slices. Sweat the Spanish onion and garlic in a medium wide-bottom saucepan with the remaining 3 tablespoons of butter. Add the arborio rice and coat with the onions and garlic. Over low heat, continue to cook, stirring constantly for 3 to 4 minutes. Add 1/4 cup of hot water or Chicken Stock to the rice and stir until completely absorbed. Continue to add hot water or Chicken Stock 1/4 cup at a time, stirring constantly and allowing the rice to completely absorb the liquid each time before adding more. Continue adding hot water or Chicken Stock 1/4 cup at a time until the rice is cooked (it should be creamy yet al dente).

Stir constantly with a smooth, gentle motion to avoid breaking the grains. Season the cooked risotto with salt and pepper and fold in the sliced leeks.

ASSEMBLY  Place the risotto in a 3-inch ring mold on the center of each plate. Remove the molds and place some of the roasted onions around the risotto. Spoon the red wine—black olive sauce around the risotto, drizzle with the Parsley Juice, and sprinkle with the reserved chopped olives. Place a mound of fried shallots on top of the risotto.

## Wine Notes

The ingredients of this dish bring Mediterranean wine and food flavors to mind. The fine Bandol Rosé by Domaine Tempier bears a complexity like no other Rosé, principally from its earthy Mourvèdre presence. Bone-dry and uniquely flavorful, it stands up to the intensity of the olives while allowing the sweet onion pleasure to persist. Another fine Rosé, from the New World, is Joseph Phelps's Grenache Rosé from California's Napa Valley. Deeper-colored and dominated by peppery Grenache, this wine is dry and refreshing, but more in the style of Tavel than of Bandol. A great olive wine.

# Collard Greens Tortellini with Bleeding Heart Radish Sauce and Smoked Tofu

*My dear friend chef Emeril Lagasse, from New Orleans, makes fantastic collard greens,
which inspired me to devise my own preparation. I use smoked tofu instead of bacon and bleeding heart
radishes, which exemplify winter. Of course, the tortellini is a different twist, but I think it
works nicely as a wonderful textural component and it makes the collard greens a more substantial dish.*

**Serves 4**

*⅔ cup chopped carrots*

*⅔ cup chopped celery*

*⅔ cup chopped Spanish onion*

*1 tablespoon grapeseed oil*

*5 bleeding heart radishes*

*Salt and pepper*

*1 bunch collard greens*

*1 tablespoon butter*

*8 ounces smoked tofu*

*½ cup plus 3 tablespoons water*

*1 teaspoon rice vinegar*

*1 portobello mushroom, roasted with cooking juices reserved*

*¾ pound Semolina Pasta (see Appendices)*

*1 small bunch flat-leaf parsley*

*1 egg yolk*

*3 cups baby red mustard greens*

METHOD Caramelize the carrots, celery, and onion with the grapeseed oil in a small rondeau. Add the whole radishes and enough water to cover the radishes by two-thirds. Bring to a simmer over medium heat, then cover and braise the radishes in the oven at 375 degrees for 1 hour, or until tender. Remove from the oven, peel the radishes, and reserve 1 cup of the braising liquid. In a blender, purée 3 of the radishes with 1 cup of the braising liquid, season with salt and pepper, and set aside. Take the remaining radishes and peel off thick layers with a paring knife, following the natural curve. Set aside. Chop the collard greens and place them in a medium saucepan with 2 teaspoons of the butter, 2 ounces of the smoked tofu, and ½ cup of water. Over low heat slowly braise the greens for 10 to 15 minutes, or until tender. Finely dice 3 ounces of the smoked tofu. Remove the greens from the pan and toss with the diced smoked tofu and the rice vinegar. Season to taste with salt and pepper. In the blender, purée the roasted portobello mushroom with ⅓ to ½ cup of the reserved cooking juices and strain through a fine-mesh sieve. Season to taste with salt and pepper.

Roll out the pasta using a pasta machine or by hand on a floured surface. Cut the parsley into a thick chiffonade. Sprinkle the parsley along half the length of the pasta and fold over the remaining pasta. Run through the pasta machine once more, or roll by hand until thin to seal the parsley in the pasta. Using a pizza cutter, cut the pasta into eight 3-inch squares. Place the yolk and 1 tablespoon of water in a small bowl and mix together to make an egg wash. Place 1 tablespoon of the collard greens mixture in the center of the square. Brush the 2 adjacent edges of the square with the egg wash and fold to a point, forming a triangle. Join the two ends of the long side of the triangle to form a tortellini. Repeat with the remaining 7 squares. Cook the tortellini in boiling salted water for 3 minutes, or until al dente. Toss with the remaining 1 teaspoon butter and season to taste with salt and pepper. Chop the remaining 3 ounces smoked tofu into batons. In a small saucepan, place 2 tablespoons of water and bring to a simmer, add the mustard greens, and gently wilt for 30 to 45 seconds. Remove from the pan and season to taste with salt and pepper.

ASSEMBLY Place a small amount of the mustard greens in the center of each plate. Set 2 tortellini vertically in the center of the mustard greens. Spoon the bleeding heart radish sauce and the wild mushroom sauce around the greens. Place a few warm radish pieces in the center of each tortellini and arrange the smoked tofu batons around the plate.

## Wine Notes

The wine choice should tie together the tartness of the collard greens and the almost baconlike smokiness of the tofu. Individually tasted, the greens are well met by the tangy acidity of a dry Savennières, but the tofu flavor is overwhelmed. The tofu is extended by a ripe, oaky Chardonnay, but this clashes with the greens. The best wine will exhibit modest oak and a slightly less ripe form, such as mountain-grown Mount Eden Estate Chardonnay or a mineral-influenced Chassagne-Montrachet by Colin-Deleger.

# Twice-Baked Yukon Gold Potatoes with White Alba Truffles

*When I think of the most decadent and satisfying flavors, a dish like this—
creamy Yukon gold potato with melted Parmesan and pungent, sensual white Alba truffles—
comes to mind. Of course, a delicious effect can be achieved with just the beautiful
Yukons and the cheese, but if you can afford to splurge, why not?*

**Serves 4**

*4 Yukon gold potatoes (about 5 to 6 ounces)*

*¼ cup heavy cream*

*2 tablespoons chopped chives, parsley,
or other fresh herbs*

*⅓ cup white truffle oil*

*½ cup grated Parmigiano-Reggiano*

*Salt and pepper*

*1 white Alba truffle, thinly sliced*

METHOD Rinse the potatoes under cold water, place on a sheet pan, and bake at 375 degrees for 45 to 60 minutes, or until soft. Remove from the oven and cool completely. Cut off the top portion of each potato, leaving two-thirds for the base (you will not need the top portion). Scoop out the inside, leaving a ¼-inch layer of the potato attached to the skin (to provide structure), and place in a medium bowl. Mix the cream, herbs, 4 tablespoons white truffle oil, and Parmesan with the large chunks of potato flesh. Season to taste with salt and pepper. Fill each potato with some of the potato mixture. Place on a sheet pan and bake at 350 degrees for 20 minutes, or until golden brown.

ASSEMBLY Place a potato on each plate, drizzle the remaining white truffle oil around the potato, and top with the white truffle slices.

**Wine Notes**

The intensity of this dish must be matched by a wine with intense, earthy aromas and flavors. The wine choice should take into account the slight bitterness of the potato skin and provide a textural foil for the creaminess of the potato in its twice-baked form. A wide range of northern white Rhones will be useful, as the Marsanne grape yields great truffle-like aromas and more earthiness as it ages. Thus, the wine should originate from a bold Hermitage producer such as Chave, although even simple Côtes du Rhône Blanc by August Clape was nearly a perfect fit. If you prefer a Hermitage, select a mature wine (at least 5 years old). A pure Marsanne wine, such as the Clape Côtes du Rhône, is at its best when young and fragrant.

# Blood Oranges with
# Warm Braised Belgian Endive,
# Missouri Black Walnuts, and Gorgonzola

*The combination of orange, Belgian endive, nuts, and blue cheese is truly incredible.
In this version I serve everything slightly warm and the effect is tremendous. With the barely warm
cheese, everything melts together beautifully. The flavors are pungent but far from overwhelming.*

**Serves 4**

*1 ¹/₂ cups freshly squeezed blood orange juice*

*¹/₃ cup chopped carrots*

*¹/₃ cup chopped onion*

*¹/₃ cup chopped celery*

*2 teaspoons grapeseed oil*

*2 heads Belgian endive*

*2 teaspoons sugar*

*4 blood oranges*

*Salt and pepper*

*¹/₂ cup chopped Missouri black walnuts*

*4 ounces Gorgonzola, at room temperature*

*1 tablespoon Herb Oil (see Appendices)*

METHOD Place the blood orange juice in a small saucepan over medium heat. Simmer for 30 to 40 minutes, or until it coats the back of a spoon.

In a wide-bottom saucepan, caramelize the carrots, onion, and celery with the grapeseed oil. Add the Belgian endive; add water mixed with the 2 teaspoons sugar to cover, filling the saucepan two-thirds full. Cover and simmer over medium heat for 15 minutes, or until tender. Remove the endive from the pan and reserve ¼ cup of the cooking liquid. Slice the blood oranges ¼ inch thick, and keeping the pulp and natural design of the orange intact, completely remove the rind and the pith. Slice the Belgian endive lengthwise into quarters. Place in a sauté pan and heat with the reserved cooking liquid. In another sauté pan, heat the blood orange slices with the reduced blood orange juice. In a large bowl, toss the endive with 2 tablespoons of the reserved cooking liquid used to reheat the endive and season with salt and pepper.

ASSEMBLY Arrange the warm blood orange slices on each plate, top with the endive, and sprinkle with the black walnuts and small chunks of the Gorgonzola. Spoon the blood orange reduction around the plate along with the remaining 2 tablespoons juice from the endive. Drizzle the Herb Oil on each plate and top with additional black pepper.

**Wine Notes**

This beautiful combination seems a tough wine match on paper, but it is remarkably wine-friendly in practice. The key is choosing a wine with sufficient acidity to align the numerous acid presences on the plate—orange and endive, and especially the tartness of blue cheese. On the other hand, the cheese flavor begs for a wine of richness with a touch of decadence. One unusual wine stands out as ideal, although it is quite rare: Lucien Crochet's Sancerre *Vendange du 25 Octobre* 1990. This late-harvest Sauvignon Blanc is an atypical Sancerre, with decidedly overripe fruit and some sweetness. Unfortunately, few wines compare with its character, so alternatives could be chosen from certain California wines like Babcock *Eleven Oaks* Sauvignon Blanc, La Jota Viognier, Caymus *Conundrum*, or even an Alsace Gewürztraminer from a ripe vintage like 1989. All of these wines offer roundness on the palate and relatively high alcohol, providing a bold counterpoint to this delicious arrangement.

# Grilled Salsify with Burdock Purée, Broccoli Raab, and Beef Stock Reduction

*Although burdock looks quite a bit like salsify and is treated and cooked much the same way, it is not quite as elegant or refined. Its flavor is a touch woodier and it is also a little more fibrous. We solve those problems by puréeing it. The beef reduction adds a potent richness to this dish and the broccoli raab contributes an earthy heartiness.*

**Serves 4**

*10 stalks salsify*

*12 stalks burdock*

*8 cups milk*

*½ cup Vegetable Stock (see Appendices)*

*2 tablespoons butter*

*Salt and pepper*

*1 teaspoon grapeseed oil*

*1 bunch broccoli raab, blanched*

*¾ cup Beef Stock Reduction (see Appendices)*

METHOD  Peel the salsify and burdock and place in separate large saucepans. Immediately add 4 cups of the milk to each pan to prevent the vegetables from oxidizing (the burdock will turn grey even in milk). Add just enough water to cover completely. Simmer over medium heat for 20 to 30 minutes, or until just tender. Drain off the milk and lightly grill both the salsify and the burdock. Coarsely chop the burdock and purée in the blender with the Vegetable Stock. Pass the burdock purée through a food mill and transfer to a medium saucepan. Over low heat, cook the burdock for 10 minutes, or until all of the excess liquid has evaporated. Fold in 1 tablespoon of the butter and season to taste with salt and pepper. Cut the salsify into 2-inch pieces on the bias, slicing the pieces in half if they are too thick. Place the salsify in a medium sauté pan with the grapeseed oil and 1 teaspoon of the butter and sauté until golden brown. Place the broccoli raab in a medium sauté pan with the remaining 2 teaspoons of butter, reheat, and season to taste with salt and pepper.

ASSEMBLY  Layer the salsify in the style of a log house, forming a square stack on each plate. Place the broccoli raab in the center of the stack. Place 4 quenelles of burdock purée around the raab on each plate, and spoon the hot Beef Stock Reduction around the salsify.

### Wine Notes

A delicate red wine seems appropriate with the beef presence in this dish. A generous sprinkling of pepper in the dish might point to a Rhône red, but the wine should have much less body and tannin than even the simplest Côtes du Rhône. Soft wines in Burgundy work much better, the best of our tastings being a Chambolle-Musigny Domaine Bertheau 1991. Vintage is all important here, as a more powerful and tannic 1990 or 1988 Burgundy would overwhelm. Another successful wine is the Chianti Classico *Badia a Passignano* 1988 by Antinori. This warm wine seems far less tannic than one might expect from Tuscany. Finally, mature Rioja Gran Reserva could also make sense from traditional bodegas such as CVNE and La Rioja Alta.

# Warm Tamarind Soup with Myer Lemon and Satsuma Mandarin Sorbet and Feijoa Chips

*Tamarind has a most unusual flavor, slightly grainy yet elegant. The sorbets are both stark but quite true to their flavors, providing a wonderful cleansing effect. The chips add texture and the preserved lemon rind supplies a sophisticated, needed sweetness. This dessert works well by itself, or as a transitional course if you want to conclude the meal with chocolate.*

**Serves 4**

*2 cups freshly squeezed Myer lemon juice (about 10 lemons)*

*6 cups Simple Syrup (see Appendices)*

*2 cups freshly squeezed Satsuma mandarin juice (about 15 mandarins)*

*1 Myer lemon, with skin, cut in small wedges*

*2 cups shelled tamarind*

*4 cups water*

*¼ cup sugar*

*5 feijoa (pineapple guava)*

METHOD To make the sorbet bases, in a mixing bowl, mix the Myer lemon juice with 2 cups of the Simple Syrup. In a separate bowl, mix the mandarin juice with 1½ cups Simple Syrup. Spin the sorbets separately in an ice cream machine until firm, and place in the freezer until ready to use.

Place the Myer lemon in a saucepan with 1½ cups Simple Syrup and simmer for 15 minutes, or until the skin is tender. Remove from heat and let cool in the syrup.

To make the tamarind soup, place the tamarind in a small saucepan and cover with the water and sugar. Simmer for about 30 minutes, or until the tamarind comes off the pit easily. Remove the pits, purée the pulp with the cooking liquid, and strain through a fine-mesh sieve. If the purée is extremely tart, adjust with the remaining Simple Syrup.

Peel the feijoa, place in a small saucepan, and cover with water. Bring to a simmer and poach for 15 to 20 minutes, or until soft. Remove from the liquid, purée in a blender, then strain through a fine-mesh sieve. On a silpat or a nonstick sheet pan, spread 30 thin quarter-size layers of the feijoa purée. Bake in the oven at 275 degrees for 15 minutes, or until dry and lightly golden in color. Carefully remove the chips from the silpat or sheet pan with a small spatula and let cool.

ASSEMBLY Place a large quenelle of each sorbet standing upright in the center of each bowl. Place the feijoa chips on top of the sorbet and ladle in the tamarind soup. Garnish with the poached Myer lemon wedges.

## Wine Notes

This light dessert is underscored by the formidable acidity of the lemon sorbet, which should be met by a high-acid sweet wine. German Eiswein comes to mind first, but choose one with some age—perhaps a 1975 or 1983. Another intensely sweet-tart possibility comes from the tiny Blackwood Canyon Winery in Washington, which occasionally makes a Trockenbeerenauslese-level wine called Pinnacle from dried, Botrytis-affected Riesling grapes. It's an incredible combination, especially with the tamarind's exotic sweetness.

Winter is most fierce as January surrenders to **February**. Invariably, it is during this month that I question my choice to live in the Midwest, but, without fail, I am reminded that life in the heart-land builds fortitude and encourages introspection. ⚜ With few distractions outside, it is especially easy to spend the month contemplating one's work. So although February can be characterized by its limited palette of foods, this is the time of year I'm most creative. I find myself thinking of legumes, mushrooms, gnocchi, slow-roasted vegetables basted in meat juices, kohlrabi, celery root, red wine reduction, nutty brown rice, and exotic spices. I use nature's limitations to my advantage and concentrate on the intellectual exercises of cooking. Consequently, I approach food as sustenance instead of art and savor flavors more acutely than at any other time of the year. In turn, I try to highlight some of the more simple and elementary flavors this month.

# Warm Portobello and Yellow-Foot Chanterelle Mushroom Terrine with Cumin-Infused Celery Root Broth

*This terrine can be prepared in advance and then heated when you are ready to serve. It requires a little work, but the result will prove worth the extra effort. The black garbanzo beans and the cumin help establish a Middle Eastern tone within the dish. By merely adding a sliced chicken breast over the top you can create a fabulous main course.*

**Serves 4**

*¹/₂ cup black garbanzo beans*

*2 cloves garlic*

*¹/₂ jalapeño*

*Salt and pepper*

*5 ounces portobello mushrooms, cleaned, stems removed, and chopped in large dice*

*3 ounces yellow-foot chanterelle mushrooms, cleaned*

*1 cup water*

*1 shallot, peeled and chopped*

*1 teaspoon butter*

*2 eggs*

*2 tablespoons chopped parsley, chives, or other fresh herbs*

*3 celery roots, peeled and juiced*

*2 teaspoons cumin seed, roasted and ground*

METHOD  Place the black garbanzo beans in a container, cover with water, and soak overnight. Drain the beans, place in a pot, and cover with water. Add the garlic and the jalapeño. Bring to a simmer and cook slowly for 3 hours, or until tender. Season to taste with salt and pepper.

Place the mushrooms in two separate oven-proof pans, with ¹/₂ cup of water in each pan; cover with aluminum foil and roast at 350 degrees for 30 minutes, or until thoroughly cooked. Purée the mushrooms separately in a blender with just enough of the cooking liquid to allow it to purée. Place the puréed mushrooms in separate saucepans and cook slowly on low heat, stirring

occasionally, until all of the excess moisture is evaporated. Remove and set aside.

In a medium sauté pan, sweat the shallot with the butter and fold into the chanterelle purée. Mix in 1 egg and season with salt and pepper. Lay flat a large piece of plastic wrap and spoon the chanterelle mixture in the middle. Fold the plastic wrap over and roll into a quarter-size cylinder. Twist the ends until the cylinder is very firm and uniformly round. Tie the ends with string. Place the chanterelle cylinder in a pot of boiling water and poach for 3 to 5 minutes, or until it bounces back to the touch and holds its shape. Remove and let cool in the plastic wrap.

Line a dome-shaped 1¹/₂ by 1¹/₂ by 5¹/₂-inch terrine mold, (other similar-size molds will also work) with plastic wrap and leave the plastic hanging over the sides. Mix the portobello mushroom purée with 1 egg and season with salt and pepper. Fill the terrine mold one-third of the way with the portobello mushroom mixture. Remove the plastic wrap from the poached yellow-foot chanterelle cylinder and gently roll it in 4 teaspoons of the chopped herbs. Place the roll in the center of the terrine mold and cover with the remaining portobello mushroom mixture. Fold the plastic wrap over the top of the terrine, place in a water bath in the oven, and bake at 350 degrees for 30 to 40 minutes, or until firm. Remove and allow to cool in the terrine mold. Juice the celery root, place the liquid in a small

saucepan, bring to a simmer, then strain through a fine-mesh sieve. Return to the saucepan with the cumin and cook over low heat for 4 minutes, then strain once more through a fine-mesh sieve.

Remove the terrine from the mold and, with the plastic wrap on, cut in ¹/₂-inch-thick slices. Before serving, remove the plastic wrap and reheat the terrine on a sheet pan in the oven at 350 degrees for 3 minutes, or until hot.

ASSEMBLY  Place 2 slices of the terrine in a bowl, scatter the black garbanzo beans around, and ladle the celery root broth around the slices. Sprinkle with the remaining 2 teaspoons chopped herbs.

## Wine Notes

We imagine this airy terrine as a first course and therefore think of light, crisp wines as appropriate matches to its delicate flavors. A fresh, racy Muscadet de Sèvre et Maine from the most recent vintage will elevate the sweet celery broth flavor and counter the slight heat of cumin. Even better, though, is crisp Champagne: several high Chardonnay versions stand out, with their citrusy freshness and (sometimes) oak influences, which are useful with mushrooms. Some producers who excel in our tastings are Deutz, Batiste-Pertois, and Veuve Clicquot *Yellow Label* Brut.

# Goat Cheese Packages with Ennis Hazelnuts, Red Wine Shallots, and Yellow Lentil Vinaigrette

*What could be better than warm goat cheese on a cold winter night?*
*With this preparation, the cheese is like butter—so meltingly soft. The Ennis hazelnuts*
*are sweet and rich and exploding with flavor. The red wine shallots*
*and the yellow lentils add depth of flavor while adding a very complex textural facet.*

**Serves 4**

*¼ cup chopped carrot*

*½ cup chopped Spanish onion*

*¼ cup chopped celery*

*1 tablespoon grapeseed oil*

*1 black radish (about 3 inches wide)*

*2 shallots, peeled and thinly sliced*

*½ cup Burgundy*

*Salt and pepper*

*½ cup yellow lentils*

*1¾ cups water*

*12 thin slices zucchini*

*⅓ cup olive oil*

*½ cup Ennis hazelnuts, toasted, peeled, and chopped*

*6 ounces goat cheese (such as Laura Chanel) cut in 1½-ounce rounds*

*1 shallot, cut in small dice*

*2 tablespoons sherry*

*1 tablespoon water*

*2 cups tatsoi greens*

*2½ cups mizuna greens*

*3 tablespoons small-diced carrot*

*3 tablespoons small-diced celery*

*3 tablespoons small-diced shiitake mushrooms*

*4 teaspoons Red Wine Reduction (see Appendices)*

METHOD Caramelize the carrot, onion, and celery in a small saucepan with 2 teaspoons of the grapeseed oil. Add the whole black radish and cover with water. In an oven-proof pan, bring to a simmer over medium heat, then cover and place in the oven at 350 degrees for 1 hour, or until tender. Remove the radish and slice thinly.

Place the sliced shallots in a small saucepan with the Burgundy and simmer over medium heat for 12 to 15 minutes, allowing the Burgundy to be absorbed by the shallots. Season to taste with salt and pepper.

Place the yellow lentils in a small saucepan and cover with 1¾ cups water. Bring to a simmer and cook very slowly for about 20 minutes, or until done. (If you boil the lentils they will break apart.)

Blanch the zucchini in boiling salted water, shock in ice water, and blot with paper towels. Lay the zucchini slices on a nonstick sheet pan, coat lightly with olive oil, and place under the broiler for 4 minutes, or until the slices are lightly browned. Lay 3 slices of zucchini, browned-side down, overlapping, on a sheet pan. Place a small mound of the hazelnuts in the center of the zucchini and place a round of the goat cheese on the hazelnuts. On the top of the goat cheese, place a spoonful of the red wine–shallot mixture and fold the two ends of the zucchini together to wrap the goat cheese. Place the sheet pan in the oven at 350 degrees for 3 to 5 minutes, or until the cheese is soft and begins to sweat.

Place the diced shallots and sherry in a bowl, slowly drizzle in the remaining olive oil, and whisk until it is incorporated. Season to taste with salt and pepper. In a sauté pan, place the water and 2 table-spoons of the sherry mixture, add the tatsoi greens and 2 cups of the mizuna greens, and gently wilt over medium heat. In a sauté pan with the remaining 1 teaspoon of grapeseed oil, sauté the carrots, celery, and

shiitake mushrooms. Toss half of the carrot mixture with the wilted greens. Toss the remaining ½ cup of the mizuna greens with 2 teaspoons of the sherry mixture and season to taste with salt and pepper. Drain any excess liquid from the lentils. In a small saucepan, toss the lentils with the remaining diced vegetables and sherry mixture. Cook over low heat until warm. Season to taste with salt and pepper.

ASSEMBLY Spoon some of the warm lentils onto each plate. Place a slice of braised black radish on top of the lentils. Top with some of the wilted greens and another slice of braised black radish. Place the zucchini-wrapped goat cheese on the radish and top with a small amount of wilted greens. Drizzle the Red Wine Reduction around the lentils.

## Wine Notes

Goat cheese brings France's Loire Valley to mind, and wines from Savennières are quite successful here. The intense, low-yielding organic vineyards of the fanatical but persuasive Nicolas Joly are all incredible statements of dry Chenin Blanc unique to their *terroir*. Clos de la Coulee de Serrant and La Roche aux Moines are the two grand cru vineyard sites that produce the most powerful wines and have the richness to fend off tatsoi's bitterness while complementing the creamy goat cheese and toasty hazelnuts. If you prefer a wine with more oaky richness, try a Pessac-Léognan from a top estate: Château Couhins-Lurton or Domaine de Chevalier Blanc are wonderful, complete, versatile wines.

# Kohlrabi Broth with Glass Noodles, Lotus Root, and Savoy Cabbage

*The flavor of kohlrabi broth is haunting. It is so simple and pure yet so completely exotic that it really makes for a startling taste experience. The glass noodles and cabbage add a heartiness to this preparation and the crispy lotus root pieces contribute a welcome crunchiness. Sometimes I even add a variety of mushrooms to this dish to make it more substantial.*

**Serves 4**

*4 cups kohlrabi juice*

*2 heads kohlrabi, peeled and thinly sliced*

*2 tablespoons butter*

*4 ounces dry Japanese glass noodles*

*2 cups savoy cabbage, cut into a thin chiffonade*

*2 teaspoons rice vinegar*

*1 lotus root, peeled and thinly sliced*

*Grapeseed oil for deep-frying*

*Salt and pepper*

*3 tablespoons sesame oil*

*8 quail eggs, hard-boiled, peeled, and thinly sliced*

METHOD Place the kohlrabi juice in a small saucepan and bring to a simmer. Once a mass has formed on top, strain through a fine-mesh sieve and set aside. Place the thinly sliced kohlrabi in a sauté pan and lightly caramelize with 1 tablespoon of the butter, about 3 to 4 minutes. Cook the noodles in boiling salted water for 7 minutes, or until al dente. Immediately shock in ice water. Place the savoy cabbage in a sauté pan and slowly cook with the remaining 1 tablespoon butter and the rice vinegar for 5 to 7 minutes, or until tender. Deep-fry the lotus root in grapeseed oil until golden brown, blot on paper towels, and season with salt. When you are ready to use the noodles, plunge them into boiling water, strain in a colander, toss with 2 tablespoons of the sesame oil, and season to taste with salt and pepper.

ASSEMBLY Place a small amount of the savoy cabbage in the bottom of each bowl. Twist some of the glass noodles into a spiral with a fork and set on top. Arrange the caramelized kohlrabi in a ring around the noodles and scatter the sliced quail eggs around the kohlrabi. Ladle the hot kohlrabi juice in each bowl and drizzle with the remaining 1 tablespoon sesame oil. Place a mound of the lotus root chips on top of the glass noodles.

## Wine Notes

This pre-meal noodle course offers aromatic pleasures as well as tactile challenge. The dominant aroma of sesame, in both oil and seed form, calls for the sweetly stimulating flavors of sake. A favorite kind is the Momokawa Gold, made with two types of polished rice. Good sake makes a delicious, light apéritif served cold. This brew also balances the slightly sweet kohlrabi broth. Those with more western tastes might prefer a crisp Oregon Pinot Gris, such as King Estate, Montinore, or Ponzi. This type of wine melds particularly well with the lotus root chips.

# Japonica Rice in Napa Cabbage with Mirliton and Kaffir Lime—Curry Broth

*I first had the incredible combination of kaffir lime and curry in a dish prepared by the brilliant New York chef, Gray Kunz. I loved the combination so much that I have worked it over and over, both in the kitchen and in my mind, experimenting with different levels of acid, sweet, and spice. This version of broth features the elegantly nutty japonica rice against the crisp, refreshing mirliton and lightly cooked napa cabbage for a subtle contrast.*

**Serves 4**

*12 large napa cabbage leaves*

*½ cup black japonica rice*

*2 cups water*

*2 tablespoons butter*

*2 mirliton (chayote), peeled*

*Salt and pepper*

*1 quart Tomato Water (see Appendices)*

*½ ounce fresh kaffir lime leaves, cut into chiffonade*

*3 tablespoons Curry Butter (see Appendices)*

METHOD Blanch the cabbage leaves in boiling salted water, shock in ice water, and pat dry. Lay the leaves flat and, with a chef's knife, remove part of the thick white inner core of the cabbage, leaving the leaf intact.

In a medium saucepan, combine the japonica rice with 2 cups of water and 1 tablespoon of the butter. Bring to a simmer and cover for about 40 minutes, or until all of the liquid is absorbed. Turn off the heat and let sit, covered, for 10 minutes.

Slice two of the mirliton ¼ inch thick, then cut the pieces into 28 round discs the size of a quarter. Finely dice the remaining mirliton, place in a sauté pan with 1 teaspoon butter, and sauté for 3 to 4 minutes. Fold into the cooked rice and season to taste with salt and pepper.

In a small saucepan, bring the Tomato Water to a simmer. Cut all of the kaffir lime leaves into a fine chiffonade, reserving 2 tablespoons for garnish, add to the Tomato Water, and steep for 3 to 4 minutes, or until the leaves begin to lose their bright green color. Strain, whisk in the Curry Butter 1 teaspoon at a time, and season to taste with salt and pepper.

Fill each of the cabbage leaves with some of the rice mixture and roll up, folding in the sides. Place on a sheet pan and bake at 350 degrees for 3 to 5 minutes, or until hot. Remove from the oven and cut off both ends. Sauté the mirliton discs in the remaining 2 teaspoons butter for 4 to 5 minutes, or until caramelized.

ASSEMBLY Place 7 of the mirliton discs in the bottom of each bowl. Place three cabbage rolls upright in the center of the discs. Ladle in the kaffir lime broth and garnish with the chiffonade of kaffir lime leaves.

### Wine Notes

Here a range of aromatically intense ingredients (mirliton, kaffir lime leaves, and curry) demand an equally aromatic wine, but one with the appropriate acidity to match the Tomato Water. Alsatian producers like Jos Meyer and Trimbach make aromatic connections with especially light Gewürztraminer and Pinot Gris. But the most successful wine, oddly, is a late harvest Sancerre from Lucien Crochet. This rarity, the *Vendange du 25 Octobre*, is made only in exceptional vintages, but is worth the search. Its richness plays well with the rice's nutty texture, and the extremely ripe style of Sauvignon Blanc carries all the aromatic intrigue of Condrieu or dry Sauternes.

# Fennel Flan with a Trio of Beans, Black Trumpet Mushrooms, and Fennel Juice Reduction

*I love slowly cooked melt-away beans in the winter, and they are a great companion to fennel, as are wild mushrooms. Here, three earthy elements come together in a very delicate yet satisfying dish.*

**Serves 4**

*¼ cup cannellini beans*

*¼ cup black turtle beans*

*¼ cup rice beans*

*2 tablespoons grapeseed oil*

*1 carrot, cut into 3 large pieces*

*1 stalk celery, cut into 3 large pieces*

*1 small Spanish onion, cut into large pieces*

*4 cloves garlic*

*2 tablespoons butter*

*Salt and pepper*

*1 large bulb fennel*

*1 cup water*

*2 eggs*

*2 egg yolks*

*6 tablespoons heavy cream*

*1 tablespoon fennel seeds, roasted*

*3 cups fresh fennel juice (about 4 to 5 heads of fennel)*

*8 bulbs baby fennel*

*7 teaspoons olive oil*

*½ cup roasted small black trumpet mushrooms (see Appendices)*

*2 oil-packed sundried tomatoes, drained and julienned*

*4 tablespoons fennel fronds*

METHOD Place the beans in 3 separate containers, cover with water, and let soak overnight. When the beans are ready, place 1 teaspoon grapeseed oil, 1 piece of the carrot and celery, and some of the onion in each of 3 separate saucepans. Over medium heat, caramelize the vegetables for 4 to 5 minutes. Drain the beans and place in the separate small saucepans with 1 garlic clove and 2 teaspoons of butter each, and cover with water. Simmer over low heat while stirring occasionally. Continue to simmer for 2 hours, or until the beans are very tender. Season to taste with salt and pepper and set aside.

Chop the large fennel bulb and mince the remaining clove of garlic. In a large sauté pan, sauté the fennel and garlic in the remaining 1 tablespoon grapeseed oil for 4 to 5 minutes, or until caramelized. Add the water and cook slowly for 30 minutes, or until tender and most of the liquid is reduced. Place the fennel mixture in a blender with the eggs and 2 yolks, heavy cream, and roasted fennel seeds. Purée on medium until smooth, strain through a fine-mesh sieve, and season with salt and pepper. Place the fennel juice in a small saucepan and simmer until it is reduced by half, about 20 minutes. Strain through a fine-mesh sieve. Rub the baby fennel with 3 teaspoons of the olive oil and roast in the oven at 400 degrees for 20 minutes, turning occasionally, until they are just caramelized and thoroughly cooked. Remove from oven, slice in half, and season to taste with salt and pepper.

Butter 4 timbale molds (1-inch-wide by 1½-inch-high timbale molds are best, but other similar-size molds will work as well) and fill with the fennel custard. (You may prepare more timbale molds if you have extra custard.) Place the molds in an ovenproof pan filled with 1 inch of water and bake at 375 degrees for 20 minutes, or until firm.

ASSEMBLY Remove the flan from the molds while still warm and place in the center of each plate. Arrange the beans and mushrooms, roasted fennel halves, and sundried tomato pieces around the flan. Spoon the fennel juice on each plate and drizzle with olive oil. Place the fennel fronds on and around each flan and top with cracked black pepper.

## Wine Notes

We return to the Rhône Valley and select Châteauneuf-du-Pape Blanc as the most effective style for the variously prepared fennel, with the right degree of ripeness to carry the creamy, rich beans. Domaine du Vieux Télégraphe provides the perfect balance and power for this complex dish because its fruit counters the ever-so-slight bitterness of the fennel.

# Rutabaga Gnocchi with Roasted Rutabaga, Wilted Sunflower Sprouts, Mushroom Juice Reduction, and Mustard Oil

*I love these smooth little melt-away dumplings. Here I simulate gnocchi with small pieces of roasted rutabaga. Roasting reinforces the wonderful, sweet flavor of this under-appreciated vegetable. The sprouts add a textural contrast, and the concentrated mushroom juice lends a potent earthiness. I like to add a couple of drops of mustard oil for a delicate zip.*

**Serves 4**

*2 pounds button mushrooms, cleaned*

*2 cups shiitake mushrooms, cleaned*

*2¹/₂ pounds rutabaga, peeled*

*Salt and pepper*

*³/₄ to 1¹/₄ cups flour*

*2 tablespoons butter*

*1 tablespoon chopped chives, parsley, or other fresh herbs*

*2 tablespoons water*

*2 cups sunflower sprouts*

*2 teaspoons Mustard Oil (recipe follows)*

*4 teaspoons roasted sunflower seeds*

METHOD Place the mushrooms in a 2¹/₂-gallon stockpot, cover with water, bring to a boil, and then reduce heat and simmer for 3 hours. Strain through a fine-mesh sieve and continue to reduce the liquid over medium heat until you have about 1¹/₂ cups of the mushroom reduction. Strain through cheesecloth and set aside.

Cut the rutabaga into twenty 1-inch-long pieces the shape of a tourne and reserve the trimmings. Dice the remaining rutabaga and place in an ovenproof dish with the trimmings from the tourned rutabaga, and cover, leaving a small hole to vent. Bake at 350 degrees for 1¹/₂ hours, or until thoroughly cooked. Purée the rutabaga in a blender and pass through a food mill. Place the purée in a nonstick sauté pan over medium heat and cook for an additional 30 to 40 minutes to reduce the excess moisture. Remove from the pan and let cool. You should have about 1 cup of purée.

To make the gnocchi, place the rutabaga in a bowl and season to taste with salt and pepper. Add the flour in small additions and mix until it doesn't stick to your fingers. (Less flour yields a more tender gnocchi.) Knead the dough for 1 minute. When you have incorporated most of the flour, divide the dough into 4 portions. On a lightly floured surface, roll each portion into a long, thin log about the diameter of a dime. Cut into ³/₄-inch-long pieces and slightly pinch the sides together. Place the gnocchi in a single layer on a floured sheet pan and refrigerate.

Place the tourned rutabaga in a sheet pan with 2 teaspoons of the butter and bake at 350 degrees for 20 minutes, turning occasionally, until golden brown. Season to taste with salt and pepper.

Drop the gnocchi in boiling salted water and cook until they begin to float (2 to 3 minutes for al dente). Remove the gnocchi and toss in a bowl with 1 tablespoon of the butter and the chopped herbs. Season to taste with salt and pepper. Place remaining 1 teaspoon butter in a small sauté pan with the water. Add the sunflower sprouts and cook over low heat for 2 minutes, or until gently wilted. Season to taste with salt and pepper.

ASSEMBLY Place the gnocchi and the roasted rutabaga in the center of each plate and top with a mound of the wilted sunflower sprouts. Spoon the mushroom reduction around the gnocchi. Drizzle the Mustard Oil around the reduction and sprinkle a few roasted sunflower seeds on each plate.

## Mustard Oil

Yield: about 1 cup

*3 tablespoons mustard seed*

*¹/₄ teaspoon turmeric*

*1 cup grapeseed oil*

METHOD Roast the mustard seeds at 350 degrees for 5 minutes. Grind the mustard seed and turmeric. Add the grapeseed oil and blend on high until completely incorporated. Store, covered, for 1 day in the refrigerator. Strain through cheesecloth, let sit for 1 more day refrigerated, and decant. Can be kept for up to 2 weeks in the refrigerator.

## Wine Notes

Toasty flavors and sweetness direct the wine choice for this very wine-friendly dish. The intensely perfumed style of Pinot Gris by two recommended Alsace producers stands out: Domaine Zind Humbrecht (the *Vieilles Vignes*) and Kuentz-Bas (the *Reserve Personelle*). These are rounder and more intense than Pinot Gris from Oregon, with the richness to match the earthy mushroom presence as well as the roasted, almost caramelized sweetness of the rutabaga gnocchi. Another favorite aromatic wine, Condrieu, seems a touch off-balance—perhaps too rich—with these flavors. A firmer, steelier style of Viognier, such as the cold-fermented version by La Jota of Howell Mountain, is a most agreeable complement.

# Flourless Chocolate Beet Cake
# with Kumquat Sorbet

*Over the years, I have enjoyed beets and chocolate in a number of different ways.
It's surprising how well the combination works. The natural sweetness of the beets cuts the
sharpness of the dark chocolate. The result is very satisfying. The kumquat is a
perfect addition to these already intriguing flavors, but orange would also work quite nicely.*

**Serves 4 to 6**

*2 1/2 cups julienned red beets*

*5 cups plus 1 tablespoon sugar*

*6 1/3 cups water*

*1 yellow beet, julienned*

*1 pound fresh kumquats*

*3 ounces dark chocolate, chopped*

*3 1/2 ounces cocoa*

*9 tablespoons butter, softened*

*3 eggs*

METHOD Place the red beets in a medium saucepan and cover with 1 cup of the sugar and 1 cup of the water. Stir and simmer over medium heat for 30 minutes. Strain, return the cooking liquid to the saucepan, and simmer over medium heat for 30 minutes, or until it coats the back of a spoon. Pour half of the beet syrup over the julienned red beets, reserving the rest for garnishing. Place the julienned yellow beet in a small saucepan with 1/2 cup of the sugar and 1 cup of the water, simmer for 30 minutes, then drain.

Poach the kumquats in boiling water for 5 minutes, drain, and repeat one more time, poaching for 10 minutes. Cut the kumquats in half and discard the pulp and seeds, reserving the peel. In a medium saucepan, combine the kumquat peels, 3 cups sugar, and 4 cups water, and simmer for 25 minutes. Remove 6 of the kumquats and julienne them for the garnish. Purée the remaining kumquats with 2 cups of the cooking liquid. Place the liquid in an ice cream machine and freeze. (If your sorbet is slightly gummy, add 1/2 cup of water and refreeze.)

In a small saucepan, bring 5 tablespoons of sugar and 1/3 cup water to a boil. Stir in the dark chocolate and the cocoa, add the butter, and stir until thoroughly combined. In the large bowl of an electric mixer, whip the eggs and 4 tablespoons of sugar to a ribbon. Fold the chocolate mixture into the whipped eggs. Fold in the julienned red beets. Butter 4 ring molds (1 1/2-inch-high by 2 1/2-inch-wide molds are best, but other molds of similar size will also work) and place on a parchment-lined sheet pan. Fill the molds three-quarters of the way with

the batter (if you have extra batter you may prepare more ring molds). Bake the cakes at 350 degrees for 20 to 25 minutes, or until just firm to the touch.

ASSEMBLY Place a cake in the center of each plate and top with the julienned yellow beet. Arrange 2 small scoops of kumquat sorbet next to them and garnish with the julienned kumquat. Drizzle the remaining red beet syrup around the plate.

## Wine Notes

The sweet beet flavor and spicy cinnamon of the beet juice make a forward, sweet fruit wine work here: Ca' Togni, a sweet red wine made from the black Hamburg (a form of Black Muscat), makes the perfect accompaniment. The chocolate flavor itself, if you choose to match it, might be best met by a fine old malmsey Madeira. Fifteen-year-old Blandy's fits well, but a rare old vintage malmsey or malvasia such as 1915 or 1922 would be a treat that carries the chocolate intensity further with its caramely richness but firm acidity.

With **March**, the mantle of dormancy is cast off and the promise of spring breathes new life into the kitchen. Before long, we are visited by the first springlike days and the season's exciting produce begins to make its way from field to market. Naturally, we hunger for the month's newest gifts, but at the same time our appetites still demand dishes with winter-strength substance. ❧ Each year, I eagerly await the challenge of making a seamless transition from the flavors of winter to the tastes of spring. Often, I enlist such stars as the delicate white eggplant, tiny white asparagus, woody morels, pepino melons, unctuous sapote, and creamy fava beans, which always perform. But while March's dishes should be slightly rich, they should also con-tain the hint of sharpness needed to arouse our diminishing appetite. Slivers of garlic chives, wisps of treviso, tart green gooseberries, and okra all serve this purpose nobly. With these dishes, you, too, will greet the changing of the seasons with heightened enthusiasm.

# Salad of Pepino Melon, Asian Pear, and Sapote with Strawberry Papaya, Mitsuba, and Key Lime–Poppy Seed Vinaigrette

*As these tropical fruits come into season, sometimes the best way to serve them is just to cut them up and dress them lightly with a vinaigrette. In this dish I have added the wonderfully refreshing mitsuba greens for a playful accent. If you omit the greens and add a pinch of sugar to the vinaigrette, you can easily turn this preparation into a light, beautiful dessert.*

**Serves 4**

*3 tablespoons Key lime juice*

*7 tablespoons olive oil*

*Salt and pepper*

*1 tablespoon poppy seeds*

*½ cup peeled and diced Asian pear*

*½ cup peeled and diced pepino melon*

*½ cup peeled and diced sapote*

*2 ounces mitsuba (about 1 cup)*

*½ cup julienned strawberry papaya*

METHOD Place the Key lime juice in a small bowl and slowly whisk in the olive oil. Season to taste with salt and pepper. Add the poppy seeds and set aside.

Gently toss the diced pear, melon, and sapote in a small bowl with 2 tablespoons of the vinaigrette. Place the mitsuba in a medium bowl, toss with 2 tablespoons of the vinaigrette, season to taste with salt and pepper, and assemble immediately.

ASSEMBLY Arrange some of the diced fruit in the center of each plate and form the mixture into a circle (you may use a 2-inch ring mold). Place individual pieces of the mitsuba and strawberry papaya around the fruit and drizzle the remaining Key lime vinaigrette around them.

## Wine Notes

The exotic sweetness of the fruits in this pretty salad demand a wine with some residual sugar but enough acid for the bitter mitsuba and the vinaigrette. Some late-harvest wines could be appropriate, even though they would generally be reserved for dessert. Vendange Tardive Gewürztraminer from Alsace is a winning style, especially the exciting Goldert Grand Cru by Zind Humbrecht. Slightly lighter and crisper are the many fine Riesling Spätlesen from the Mosel or Saar— Wehlener Sonnenuhr, Urziger Würzgarten, Graacher Himmelreich—from great producers like J. J. Prüm, Dr. Loosen, and Willi Schaefer. Other useful wines are made in the Demi-Sec style by the great Champagne firms: Moët et Chandon and Veuve Clicquot Demi-Sec would be sparkling choices with this plate served as an early brunch course.

# Morels with Yellow Corn Grits, Okra, and Morel Juices

~~~~~~~~~~~~~~~~~~~~~~~~~~~~~~~~~~~~~~~~~~~~~~~~~~~~~~~~~~~~~~~~~~~~~~~~~~~~~~~~~~~~~~~~~~~~~~~

*There is nothing like the first morels of the season. They are unequivocally*
*my favorite mushroom, and they are among the most earthy foodstuffs I know.*
*Here the morels are stuffed with yellow corn grits and cooked with okra.*
*The mushroom juices are flavored with thyme and a drizzle of olive oil.*
*Very simple to prepare, and very easy to serve!*
*It is hard for me to think of a more profound combination of flavors.*

**Serves 4**

*8 morel mushrooms*

*5 sprigs thyme*

*3 tablespoons extra virgin olive oil*

*Salt and pepper*

*1 cup water*

*1 cup hot cooked yellow corn grits*

*8 whole okra, blanched*

METHOD  Place the morel mushrooms in an ovenproof pan with 1 sprig of the thyme, 1 tablespoon of the olive oil, salt and pepper to taste, and water. Cover and bake at 350 degrees for 30 to 40 minutes, or until done.

Remove the mushrooms and reserve the liquid in the pan. Pour the morel juices in a small saucepan. Simmer over medium heat, for 3 to 4 minutes, or until reduced by one-third. Slice the morels in half lengthwise and fill 12 halves with the hot cooked grits. In a small sauté pan, warm the okra in a few teaspoons of water and slice into 1/4-inch pieces. Season to taste with salt and pepper.

ASSEMBLY  Place a small amount of okra in the center of each plate. Place 3 of the stuffed morels on top of the okra along with 1 plain morel half. Place 1 sprig of thyme on each plate and spoon the reduced morel juices over the mushrooms. Drizzle the remaining 2 tablespoons olive oil around the plate.

### Wine Notes

A tangy Sauvignon Blanc from California provides refreshment for this preparation, as sweet corn flavors are well balanced by Sauvignon's acidity. We like the Babcock *Eleven Oaks* for its richness and balance. It also cuts through the viscous consistency of the okra. Some white Burgundy and California Chardonnays are also effective if oak is a background element.

# White Eggplant Soup with Pickled Baby Eggplant and Basil Oil

*This soup is very simple, but incredibly flavorful. The satiny presence of the roasted eggplant is offset by the poignant flavors of the pickled eggplant and the garlic chives. Finally, the addition of the Basil Oil gives it a perfect richness.*

**Serves 4**

*6 white eggplant*

*1 tablespoon olive oil*

*Salt and pepper*

*3 cups water*

*1 cup Pickling Juice (see Appendices)*

*8 baby purple eggplant*

*1 tablespoon yellow garlic chives, sliced on the bias*

*1 tablespoon green garlic chives, sliced on the bias*

*Basil Oil (see Appendices)*

METHOD Slice the white eggplant in half, rub lightly with olive oil, and season with salt and pepper. Place on a sheet pan, skin side up. Pour 1 cup of the water into the sheet pan and roast the eggplant in the oven at 350 degrees for 45 to 55 minutes, or until soft. Scoop out the eggplant pulp and discard the skin. Place the pulp in the blender and purée with the remaining 2 cups of water. Strain through a fine-mesh sieve and season with salt and pepper.

Bring the Pickling Juice to a simmer and add the baby eggplant. Turn off the heat and let sit at room temperature for at least 2 hours in the Pickling Juice. Refrigerate until needed.

ASSEMBLY Ladle the warm soup into each of the bowls. Slice the pickled eggplant and place in the center of the bowl. Sprinkle with the garlic chives and drizzle with Basil Oil.

**Wine Notes**

The piquancy of the pickling spices intensifies the tart eggplant flavor in this "meaty" soup. The snappy and pungent La Gitana Manzanilla Sherry by Hidalgo would make a lively early course companion. More smoky sherry can be found in Puerto, where both Osborne and Lustau make excellent, robust fino styles. Champagne can also be useful with soup, as it adds a textural element (more specifically, effervescence) to the smooth, rich purée. R de Ruinart proves an elegant, well-matched flavor, with high acidity neutralizing the Pickling Juice tartness.

# Cardoon Lasagne with Caramelized Onion and Fava Bean Sauce

*I first read about cardoon in Fernand Points's* Ma Gastronomic, *and I have been
intrigued by this artichokelike thistle ever since. In this preparation
I have added a perfect companion to the cardoon in the form of a heady fava bean sauce.
This would also work well if the cardoon was incorporated into ravioli and then served with the
fava beans. The lasagne, though, is a very elegant way to serve these tremendous foods.*

## Serves 4

*12 stalks of cardoon*

*Juice of 1 lemon*

*Water*

*2 cups chopped carrots*

*2 cups chopped Spanish onions*

*4 teaspoons grapeseed oil*

*Salt and pepper*

*1 large Spanish onion, peeled*

*³/4 pounds Semolina Pasta (see Appendices)*

*2 cups fava beans, blanched and peeled*

*2 tablespoons olive oil*

*¼ cup Parsley Juice (see Appendices)*

*2 teaspoons butter*

*1 tablespoon chopped fresh parsley, chives,
or other herbs*

*1 tablespoon chopped fresh tarragon*

METHOD Peel the cardoon, cut it into 2-inch pieces, and immediately place it in a large container with the lemon juice and enough water to cover. In a large saucepan, caramelize the chopped carrots and onions with 2 teaspoons of the grapeseed oil. Add the cardoon and cover with water. Simmer over medium heat for 3 hours, or until the cardoon is tender. Purée half of the cooked cardoon in a blender and pass through a food mill. Place the purée in a small saucepan, and over low heat, reduce for 30 minutes, or until the purée thickens. Season to taste with salt and pepper and keep warm.

Cut the onion in half and then into thirds lengthwise. Separate the onion pieces and place in a medium sauté pan with the remaining 2 teaspoons of grapeseed oil. Over medium heat, caramelize the onion and set aside. Using a pasta machine, or by hand, roll out the pasta until thin, and cut into 16 (2½ x 1-inch) pieces. Place half of the fava beans in a blender and purée with 4 teaspoons of the olive oil. Add the Parsley Juice and season to taste with salt and pepper. Strain through a fine-mesh sieve and warm just prior to use. Place the remaining fava beans in a small saucepan with 2 teaspoons of the olive oil, warm over low heat, and season to taste with salt and pepper. Cook the pasta in boiling salted water until al dente. Toss with the butter, chopped herbs, and tarragon, and season with salt and pepper.

ASSEMBLY Place a piece of cardoon, some of the cardoon purée, and 2 pieces of the caramelized onion in the center of each plate and top with a piece of pasta. Repeat until you have 4 layers. Place a piece of the caramelized onion on top of the lasagne and place a few fava beans around the lasagne. Spoon some of the warm fava bean sauce around the edge of the plates.

## Wine Notes

The earthy flavors of this arrangement lead to a wine with a touch of oakiness. Mature white Burgundy makes an excellent match. An example is any Domaine Leflaive Puligny-Montrachet from 1989 (or even back to 1985 or 1986 vintage). Wines with little or no oak aromas and flavors can also work, such as Clos de la Coulee de Serrant 1991, as they are an earthy match with these root vegetables. Pinot Gris from Zind-Humbrecht adds richness to the finishing aniselike flavors of both food and wine.

# Ragout of Baby Bok Choy, Haricots Verts, Yellow Wax Beans, and Dragon's Tongue Beans with Japanese Cucumber Sauce

*This preparation emphasizes the differences in flavors and textures between the three*
*types of beans and marries them with the delicious flavors of Japanese cucumber and bok choy.*
*The flavors are simultaneously rustic and refined.*
*The dish is very light and will work well in a multicourse dinner.*

**Serves 4**

*5 Japanese cucumbers*
*2 tablespoons butter*
*1 cup water*
*Salt and pepper*
*4 baby bok choy*
*28 haricots verts, blanched*
*20 yellow wax beans, blanched*
*8 dragon's tongue beans, blanched*
*2 tablespoons Herb Oil (see Appendices)*
*4 teaspoons chopped chervil*

METHOD Place 2 of the cucumbers in a large sauté pan with the butter, water, and salt and pepper to taste. Cover and slowly braise for 10 minutes, or until tender. Add the bok choy and cook for 3 minutes, then add the beans and continue cooking for 2 minutes, or until al dente. Slice the cooked cucumber into 2-inch-long pieces and quarter them. Purée the remaining cucumbers and pass through a sieve, allowing some of the pulp to pass through. Just prior to serving, warm the cucumber sauce in a small saucepan over low heat while whisking in the Herb Oil. Season to taste with salt and pepper.

ASSEMBLY Lay the bok choy in the center of each plate. Top with wedges of cucumber and some of the beans. Spoon the cucumber sauce around the bok choy. Spoon some of the hot cooking liquid on top of the beans and sprinkle with the chopped chervil.

## Wine Notes

This dish needs a delicate wine with little or no oak presence. Greens seem to need tart Sauvignon, but beans can handle a bit more richness in the wine. American Sauvignon Blanc makes the most sense, as Loire Valley versions can be too austere and Italian ones too aggressive. Producers who use only older oak for the maturation of their Sauvignon Blanc will provide elegant yet slightly toasty wines for this light plate. We like Duckhorn best of the many tasted.

# Green and Tiny White Asparagus with Hearts of Palm, Purslane, Treviso, and Marcona Almonds

*This is a very refreshing combination of ingredients. In fact, it is a great way to signal that spring is on the way. The Marcona almonds from Spain add a glorious sweetness which acts as the thread that ties together all of the dish's distinctive flavors.*

## Serves 4

*1 shallot, diced*

*¼ cup rice vinegar*

*½ cup olive oil*

*Salt and pepper*

*1 tablespoon freshly squeezed lemon juice*

*1 cup water*

*1½ cups julienned hearts of palm*

*1 cup green asparagus tips, blanched and cut in half*

*7 ounces tiny white asparagus, blanched*

*¼ cup treviso, julienned*

*3 cups loosely packed purslane*

*¼ cup Marcona almonds, roasted and sliced*

METHOD Combine the shallot and the rice vinegar in a small bowl. Slowly whisk in the olive oil and season to taste with salt and pepper.

Combine the lemon juice and water in a large bowl, add the hearts of palm, and let sit for 30 minutes. Drain, then add the green and white asparagus, treviso, and purslane. Toss with about half of the vinaigrette and season to taste with salt and pepper.

ASSEMBLY Place a high mound of the asparagus mixture in the center of each plate. Spoon the remaining vinaigrette on top of the asparagus and sprinkle the almonds around the plate.

## Wine Notes

The most effective wine choice here is an oakier style of Sauvignon Blanc, perhaps aided by the blending of Sémillon or other richer varieties. This variety is great for the asparagus, and oakiness helps amplify the almond flavor. The natural first option with this in mind is Graves or other white Bordeaux. However, these wines can seem too rich in some instances—Blanc de Lynch Bages and Château La Louviere are successful though perhaps a touch rich and smoky. Joseph Phelps and Duckhorn are two Napa Valley Sauvignon Blancs that rely on just a kiss of oak, with enough refreshing structure to keep the palate stimulated. Because they are slightly leaner than the Bordeaux, they are more successful with the tart components of this lovely salad.

# Cardamom-Carrot Griddle Cakes with Warm Cape Gooseberries and Tahitian Vanilla Bean Ice Cream

~~~~~~~~~~~~~~~~~~~~~~~~~~~~~~~~~~~~~~~~~~~~~~~~~~~~~~~~~~~~~~~~

*I like the combination of cardamom and carrot because they work well together in savory*
*or dessert preparations. Pairing these flavors always reminds me of a Middle Eastern dessert*
*I ate while exploring pastry shops in Jerusalem. Here I have delicate little pancakes*
*served with the ever-so-slightly tart Cape gooseberries and a not-too-sweet vanilla ice cream.*
*This dessert would be nice for a sophisticated dinner party.*

**Serves 4 to 6**

*1 egg*

*1 cup milk*

*3 tablespoons butter, melted*

*1/2 teaspoon salt*

*1/2 teaspoon baking soda*

*1/2 cup plus 1 1/2 tablespoons sugar*

*3/4 cup flour*

*2 cups grated carrots*

*1 tablespoon ground cardamom*

*1/2 cup water*

*1 vanilla bean*

*2 pints Cape gooseberries*

*Tahitian Vanilla Bean Ice Cream*
*(recipe follows)*

METHOD Combine the egg, milk, and butter in a medium bowl. Stir in the salt, baking soda, 1/2 cup of the sugar, and the flour. Fold in the carrots and cardamom. In a medium nonstick sauté pan over medium heat, drop the batter into the pan 1 tablespoon at a time until the pan is full. Cook the griddle cakes for 2 minutes, or until golden, flip over, and continue cooking until both sides of the griddle cakes are golden. Remove and keep warm. Repeat until you have 20 small griddle cakes. In a medium saucepan over medium heat, combine the remaining 1 1/2 tablespoons sugar and the water and bring to a simmer. Split the vanilla bean lengthwise and scrape the pulp into the saucepan. Add the vanilla bean pod and the gooseberries, and cook for 2 minutes, or until hot. Remove the thin skin from the berries and discard.

ASSEMBLY Place 5 griddle cakes, overlapping, in the center of each plate. Spoon the gooseberries around the cakes along with some of the vanilla syrup they were cooked in. Place two small scoops of the ice cream on top of the griddle cakes.

## Tahitian Vanilla Bean Ice Cream

Yield: 1 quart

*1 1/2 cups heavy cream*
*3/4 cup milk*
*3/4 cup half-and-half*
*3 Tahitian vanilla beans*
*6 egg yolks*
*3/4 cup plus 2 tablespoons sugar*

METHOD Combine the heavy cream, milk, and half-and-half in a medium saucepan. Split the vanilla bean pods lengthwise and scrape out the pulp into the cream mixture. Bring to a boil over medium heat. Whisk the yolks and the sugar together in a medium bowl, temper with the hot cream, and return the mixture to the saucepan. Cook over medium heat for 2 minutes, stirring constantly. Strain through a fine-mesh sieve. Cool, then freeze in an ice cream machine.

### Wine Notes

Though the gooseberries are quite tart, balancing the sweet carrot and vanilla ice cream flavors, the overall sense of this dessert is aromatically arousing and sweetly satisfying. The wine should convey the same. On its own or with the dish, the Bonny Doon Muscat Canelli *Vin de Glaciere* is one of the most hedonically thrilling wines we know, with in-your-face apricot and peach perfume and brain-tingling sweetness. It fares better than Sauternes, Tokaji, or Eiswein, all of which require more earthbound flavors on the plate than this magical combination.

In *Waste Land,* T.S. Eliot wrote that "**April** is the cruelest month." Surely he was not much of a gastronome because April is indeed most kind when it comes to things to eat. ❧ To start with, the most lordly vegetable of all, asparagus, is in all its glory. And baby wild leeks, known as ramps, begin to push up through their earthen ceiling. Also available in abundance are hedgehog mushrooms, English peas, yellow plum tomatoes, yellow squash and their blossoms, greens, and fennel, along with one of my all-time favorite vegetables—rhubarb. Although we are attracted to lighter foods as the weather warms, April's brisk evenings cannot be denied. Fortunately, a legion of ideal foods are easily procured this time of year. Grains and legumes show off their versatility, an Asian-influenced broth works perfectly any time of the day, and my rich vegetable "cannelloni" helps ward off the chill. Surely the flavors and textures of April's produce will convince you that it cannot possibly be "the cruelest month."

# Eggplant and Potato "Cannelloni" with Wilted Spinach and Cardamom-Carrot Juice

*This faux cannelloni works beautifully by itself or as an accompaniment to meat or fish.*
*The combination of potato, eggplant, and cardamom is truly a seamless match.*
*The spinach and the onion sprouts add a perfect foil for the rich eggplant and the sweet carrot flavor.*
*They also provide a nice textural contrast.*

**Serves 4**

*2 extra large Idaho potatoes, peeled*

*1/2 cup butter, melted*

*2 Japanese eggplants (about 3/4 pound), peeled*

*4 tablespoons olive oil*

*Salt and pepper*

*2 cups julienned Spanish onion*

*1 clove garlic, chopped*

*1/2 cup carrot juice*

*2 teaspoons rice vinegar*

*4 teaspoons Cardamom Oil (recipe follows)*

*7 teaspoons Vanilla Oil (recipe follows)*

*1 tablespoon butter*

*2 tablespoons water*

*2 cups baby spinach, cleaned*

*1/4 cup onion sprouts*

*1/4 cup red clover sprouts*

METHOD Cut each potato into a large rectangle. Using a mandoline, slice thinly along the widest and longest part of the potato. You will need 16 slices. Brush both sides of the potato slices with the melted butter. Place on a sheet pan lined with parchment paper and bake in the oven at 350 degrees for 10 minutes to soften the potato. Chop the eggplant into 1 1/2-inch batons, toss with 2 tablespoons of the olive oil, and season with salt and pepper; roast in the oven at 350 degrees for 10 to 15 minutes, or until tender. In a medium sauté pan, place the remaining 2 tablespoons olive oil, the onions, and garlic, and cook over medium heat for 10 to 15 minutes, or until caramelized. Season to taste with salt and pepper and set aside. Place the carrot juice in a small saucepan and simmer for 5 minutes; strain through a fine-mesh sieve and let cool. Place the carrot juice in a blender and, while on medium, slowly add the rice vinegar, Cardamom Oil, and Vanilla Oil. Blend until completely emulsified and season to taste with salt and pepper.

Lay 2 of the potato pieces side by side overlapping 1/4 inch and season with salt and pepper. In the center of each potato, place some of the roasted eggplant and caramelized onion, roll up, and return to the parchment-lined sheet pan. Repeat this step 7 more times. Place in the oven at 400 degrees for 10 to 15 minutes, or until golden brown. Place 1 tablespoon butter and the water in a medium saucepan and quickly wilt the spinach over medium heat. Remove from the pan and season to taste with salt and pepper.

ASSEMBLY Place some of the spinach and 2 of the potato cannelloni in the center of each plate. Spoon the cardamom-carrot sauce around the plate and top the cannelloni with some of the onion and clover sprouts.

## Cardamom Oil

Yield: about 1 cup

*1/2 cup roasted cardamom seeds, in husks*

*1 cup grapeseed oil*

METHOD Place the cardamom and grapeseed oil in a blender and grind until the cardamom is incorporated into the oil. Pour into a container, cover, and let sit until most of the sediment has settled. When ready to use, ladle the oil off the top without disturbing the sediment that has settled. Can be kept for up to 2 weeks in the refrigerator.

## Vanilla Oil

Yield: 1 cup

*2 vanilla beans*

*1 cup grapeseed oil*

METHOD Split the vanilla beans lengthwise and scrape their pulp into a blender. Add the oil and purée until incorporated. Pour into a container, add the vanilla bean pods, and let sit covered for 1 day before using the oil. Can be kept for 2 weeks in the refrigerator.

## Wine Notes

The wine recommendation for this recipe depends on the intensity of the cardamom and the sweetness of the carrot sauce. If it is subdued, mildly oaky wines from Burgundy are the most interesting: Puligny-Montrachet from a good producer like Louis Carillon carries the potato and eggplant richness while maintaining the acidity to match the greens. If the sweet spiciness of the sauce is emphasized, pair it with a spicy Gewürztraminer from Alsace. Kuentz-Bas makes a great one for this dish from the *Pfersigberg* Grand Cru vineyard.

# Miso—Egg Drop Soup with Seaweed Dumplings and Ramps

~~~~~~~~~~~~~~~~~~~~~~~~~~~~~~~~~~~~~~~~~~~~~~~~~~~~~~~~~~

*This version of Egg Drop Soup was inspired by Bill Kim, one of my sous chefs.*
*The seaweed dumplings explode with flavor, and the ramps and daikon sprouts add a wonderfully*
*refreshing dimension. The heat can be controlled with more or less chile paste and jalapeño,*
*and the acid can be adjusted by altering the quantity of rice vinegar. Furthermore, by merely adding*
*some slices of seared tuna, or some poached salmon, this becomes a substantial dish.*

**Serves 4**

*8 cups plus ³/₄ cup water*

*2 tablespoons chopped gingerroot*

*2 tablespoons chopped lemongrass*

*2 tablespoons red miso*

*1 jalapeño, chopped*

*2 tablespoons tamari soy sauce*

*2 tablespoons hoisin paste*

*1 teaspoon chile paste*

*Salt and pepper*

*2 tablespoons rice vinegar*

*1 teaspoon sugar*

*4 tablespoons minced carrots*

*¹/₂ cup seaweed salad*

*16 wonton wrappers, cut into 2-inch squares*

*1 tablespoon butter*

*16 ramps, cleaned*

*1 sheet nori, cut into thin chiffonade*

*2 tablespoons sesame oil*

*1 egg, lightly beaten*

*4 tablespoons daikon sprouts*

METHOD Place 8 cups of the water, the ginger, lemongrass, red miso, and jalapeño in a large saucepan and simmer for 30 minutes. Strain and return to the pot. Add the tamari, hoisin, and chile paste and season to taste with salt and pepper. Place the rice vinegar, sugar, and carrots in a small saucepan. Simmer until all of the liquid is absorbed. Coarsely chop the seaweed salad and add it to the carrots.

In the center of each wonton, place a small amount of the seaweed salad mixture. Lightly brush the edges of the wontons with water and fold up all 4 corners to a point. Gently press together to seal the wontons. In a large sauté pan, place the butter and the remaining ³/₄ cup water, bring to a simmer, and add the ramps. Simmer gently for 3 to 4 minutes, or until tender. Season to taste with salt and pepper. Just prior to assembly, place the wontons in boiling salted water and cook for 2 to 3 minutes, or until al dente. Toss the wontons with the nori and 2 teaspoons of the sesame oil. Season to taste with salt and pepper. Bring the broth to a boil and gently stir in the egg. Remove from heat and use immediately.

ASSEMBLY Place 4 ramps, 4 wontons, and some of the daikon sprouts in the center of each bowl. Ladle in the soup. Drizzle with the remaining 4 teaspoons sesame oil.

## Wine Notes

Texture and aroma make Champagne the best wine selection, especially a toasty, long-on-the-lees style. We like the hard-to-find Batiste-Pertois, a Champagne produced by a grower who sells most of his Chardonnay to Mumm, but bottles a small amount of wine under his own label. This handmade, old-fashioned Champagne is toasty and rich, yet appropriately refreshing with the heat of the soup and the nutty sesame oil presence. Easier to find is the Mumm de Cramant, also solely Chardonnay from Cramant in Champagne.

# Yellow Squash and Jicama Soup with Jalapeño, Red Chiles, and Squash Blossoms

~~~~~~~~~~~~~~~~~~~~~~~~~~~~~~~~~~~~~~~~~~~~~~~~~~~~~~~~~~~~~~~~~~~~~

*The idea for this soup originally came from a suggestion from my assistant Sari Zernich.*
*The moment it was served, I fell in love with it. The soup*
*combines hot, sweet, creamy, spicy, and herbaceous. Everything melds together*
*perfectly into a preparation that is at the same time elegant and casual.*
*The quantity of the small red finger chiles can be controlled for the desired zing.*

## Serves 4

*1 cup chopped Spanish onion*

*1 tablespoon olive oil*

*3 cups yellow squash, cut into a large dice*

*2 cups jicama, peeled and cut into a large dice*

*2 jalapeño peppers, minced*

*2 cups plus 1 tablespoon water*

*1 teaspoon turmeric*

*Salt and pepper*

*2 tablespoons crème fraîche*

*3 tablespoons chopped primroses*

*6 squash blossoms, julienned*

*2 red finger chile peppers, thinly sliced*

*1/4 cup jicama, peeled and cut into a small dice*

*1 tablespoon chopped fresh tarragon*

*Tarragon Oil (see Appendices)*

METHOD Sauté the onion with 1 tablespoon olive oil in a medium saucepan until translucent, about 3 to 5 minutes. Add the yellow squash, jicama, 1 of the jalapeños, and 2 cups of the water. Bring to a simmer, add the turmeric, and cook for 30 to 40 minutes. Place the squash mixture in the blender and purée until smooth. Strain through a fine-mesh sieve and season to taste with salt and pepper. In a small bowl, combine the crème fraîche and the remaining 1 tablespoon water and gently fold in 2 tablespoons of the primroses.

ASSEMBLY Ladle some of the squash soup in each bowl. In the center of the soup, place a mound of the squash blossoms, the remaining primroses, some of the red chile peppers, the remaining jalapeño, the diced jicama, and the tarragon. Drizzle the crème fraîche and Tarragon Oil around the soup.

**Wine Notes**

This brilliant soup is unabashedly hot and requires a wine that will not emphasize heat with high alcohol. We find the fruit intensity of Muscat ideal with the slightly sweet/hot aromas of the soup and the visual floral suggestion of the blossoms. But the style of Alsace or Styrian Muscat is too rich and high in alcohol. More appropriate is the very light, slightly fizzy, delightfully sweet Moscato d'Asti of the Piemonte: at 5.5 percent alcohol and 5 to 7 percent residual sugar, this wine is light, refreshing, and delicious in a straightforward way. Try versions by Rivetti, Saracco, or Chiarlo. Andrew Quady makes a similar wine in California called Electra, as does Bonny Doon in the Ca' del Solo label.

# Roasted Beet, Asparagus, and Goat Cheese Terrine with Mâche, Dill, and 28-Year-Old Balsamic Vinegar

*I love the combined flavors of asparagus, goat cheese, and beets. The elements in this dish all marry perfectly to create a flavor that is both earthy and elegant. The dill adds a delicate surprise, while the aged balsamic adds just the right touch of acid. As with many of my terrines, you could simply forego the whole molding process and toss the ingredients like a salad.*

**Serves 4 to 6**

*³/₄ cup red beet juice*

*2 large red beets*

*1 bunch spinach, cleaned and blanched*

*36 long thin asparagus spears, blanched*

*4 ounces goat cheese (such as Coach Farm)*

*1 shallot, peeled and chopped*

*Salt and pepper*

*1 tablespoon water*

*1 tablespoon fresh dill*

*3 tablespoons Dill Oil (see Appendices)*

*1 cup loosely packed mâche leaves*

*2 tablespoons 28-year-old balsamic vinegar*

METHOD  Place the beet juice in a small saucepan over medium heat and simmer for 15 to 20 minutes, or until reduced to about ¼ cup. Strain through a fine-mesh sieve and set aside. Place the whole beets in a baking pan and roast in the oven at 350 degrees for 2 hours, or until tender. Peel the roasted beets and slice thin, leaving whole pieces. Cut 6 or more of the beet slices the width of the terrine mold and trim the edges to square them off. Lay 3 or more of the pieces in a row end to end to form a rectangle. Place a second layer of beets on top of the first layer. Blot both sides of the beets with paper towels. Wrap the beets in a few of the spinach leaves and set aside.

Cut the tips off the asparagus, making all of the spears about 4 inches long; reserve the tips for later use. Place 3 ounces of the goat cheese in a bowl, add the shallot, and stir until combined.

Line a terrine mold with plastic wrap. Spread a thin layer of goat cheese on the bottom, lay about 6 spears of asparagus side by side in the mold and season with salt and pepper. Spread another thin layer of goat cheese on top of the asparagus and press firmly, making sure the goat cheese has fallen between the asparagus, holding it in place. Repeat this until you have 3 layers of asparagus. Place the spinach-wrapped beets in the terrine on top of the asparagus. Place another layer of asparagus on top of the beets and continue with layering the goat cheese and asparagus until you have 3 more layers. Fold the plastic wrap over and place in the refrigerator for at least 2 hours.

Spread out a sheet of plastic wrap and place the thinly sliced beets in a layer slightly overlapping each other to form a 4 by 8-inch rectangle. Continue until the layer is the length of the asparagus terrine and triple its width. Blot the beets with paper towels. Lightly blot the remaining spinach with paper towels and lay it flat on top of the beets, making sure all of the beets are covered with the spinach leaves. Remove the terrine from the mold and discard the plastic wrap. Place the terrine on the bottom edge of the spinach-beet wrap. Trim the edges of the beet and spinach to match the length of the terrine. Roll the terrine in the beet wrap while pulling away the plas-

tic wrap with each turn. Once the terrine is completely wrapped with the beets, cover tightly with plastic wrap and place in the refrigerator.

Mix the remaining goat cheese with the water until smooth; this is the goat cheese cream. Place the asparagus tips and dill in a small bowl, toss with 1 tablespoon Dill Oil and season to taste with salt and pepper. Just prior to assembly, slice the terrine with the plastic wrap left on. Remove the plastic wrap before serving.

ASSEMBLY  Place one slice of the terrine in the center of each plate. At the top of the terrine lay 6 or 7 mâche leaves and a small amount of the asparagus tips and dill salad. Spoon a small amount of the goat cheese cream on each plate and drizzle the remaining 2 tablespoons Dill Oil, the balsamic vinegar, and beet reduction around.

**Wine Notes**

Loire Valley whites seem logical for these ingredients. A crisp Sancerre is a natural match for zesty goat cheese and the always problematic (for wine) asparagus, and it provides an excellent foil for the sweetness of beet juice. Lucien Crochet's *La Croix du Roy* is a fine example, not too racy, but still lively and assertively Sauvignon. Crisp whites from northern Italy can work as well; the full-blown style of Puiatti's Sauvignon or Pinot Bianco creates similar effects to those of Sancerre.

# Olive Oil–Poached Yellow Roma Tomatoes with English Peas, Hedgehog Mushrooms, and Pea and Tomato Juices

*The first sign of peas fantastically signals the onset of spring.*
*Here I have combined them with luscious olive oil–poached yellow Roma tomatoes and the*
*very earthy hedgehog mushrooms. Pea and tomato juices not only reinforce the*
*flavors but add a wonderfully smooth texture, while the sage blossoms add a piquant accent.*

**Serves 4**

*6 yellow Roma tomatoes*
*2 cups plus 2 tablespoons olive oil*
*1 sprig rosemary*
*1½ cups cleaned and blanched English peas*
*¼ cup water*
*3 tablespoons Parsley Juice (see Appendices)*
*Salt and pepper*
*2 tablespoons butter*
*1 shallot, chopped*
*1 cup roasted hedgehog mushrooms*
*¼ cup chopped parsley, chives, or other herbs*
*12 sage blossoms*

METHOD Remove the core from the tomatoes, leaving them whole. Place them standing upright in an ovenproof dish just large enough to hold them. Add 2 cups of the olive oil and the rosemary, and cover. Bake at 275 degrees for 3 to 4 hours, or until the skin easily comes off the tomato. Let cool, then remove the skin and seeds from the tomatoes. Strain the olive oil and let sit for 15 minutes. Using a ladle, carefully decant the olive oil. Discard the water from the tomatoes that has settled on the bottom of the pan.

Place ½ cup of the English peas in a blender with the ¼ cup water and the remaining 2 tablespoons olive oil. Blend on medium until smooth. Strain through a fine-mesh sieve, add the Parsley Juice, and season to taste with salt and pepper. Place in the refrigerator until needed. Place ¾ cup of the tomatoes in the blender with 3 tablespoons of the reserved olive oil and purée until smooth. Strain, and season to taste with salt and pepper. Place 1 tablespoon of the butter and the shallot in a medium sauté pan and sauté over medium heat until translucent. Add the hedgehog mushrooms and sauté over medium heat for 3 to 4 minutes, or until hot. Season to taste with salt and pepper. Place the remaining yellow tomatoes in a small saucepan and, over medium heat, cook until hot. Season to taste with salt and pepper. In a small saucepan over medium heat, cook the remaining 1 cup English peas with the remaining 1 tablespoon butter until hot. Fold in the herbs and season to taste with salt and pepper.

ASSEMBLY Place a 2-inch ring mold (any similar-size mold will also work) in the center of each plate. Place a layer of the English peas in the mold. Next, top with a layer of the tomatoes, then another layer of peas, and top with the hedgehog mushrooms. Scatter 3 of the sage blossoms on top of the mushrooms. Spoon some of the yellow tomato purée and English pea juice around each plate.

**Wine Notes**

The initial reaction after reading this spring recipe, full of gently tart yet sweet elements, is to look to the Loire Valley, where fresh Sauvignon and Chenin Blanc abound. Sage, however, demands a more powerful wine match, so we find Rhône whites more practical. Château de Fonsalette Blanc, made by the estimable J. Reynaud at Château Rayas, is a fine dry and firm wine for the dish. Other Marsanne-based wines, from St. Joseph, Hermitage, and even simple Côtes du Rhône Blanc, would also be practical.

# Brown Basmati Rice with Roasted Fennel, Braised Leeks, Red Wine Sauce, and White Truffle Oil

*I love the nutty flavor and toothsome texture of basmati. This dish brings together the
elegant flavor of the rice with red wine, fennel, leek, and white truffle oil.
The result is a balanced combination of four distinctly sophisticated flavors. This preparation can be
served as is, or a slice of duck breast can be draped over the top for a fantastic effect.*

**Serves 4**

*1/2 cup chopped Spanish onion*

*1/2 cup chopped carrots*

*1/2 cup chopped celery*

*1 tablespoon grapeseed oil*

*1 large leek, cleaned*

*3 tablespoons butter*

*3/4 cup fennel juice*

*1 fennel bulb, roasted*

*1 1/2 cups hot cooked brown basmati rice*

*1/4 cup chopped fennel fronds*

*Salt and pepper*

*1 cup small-diced fennel*

*1/4 cup Red Wine Reduction
(see Appendices)*

*4 teaspoons white truffle oil*

METHOD  In a saucepan over medium heat, caramelize the onion, carrots, and celery with the grapeseed oil. Cut the leek into two 2-inch-long portions, and cut each piece in half lengthwise. Tie the leeks together with string and place in the saucepan with the caramelized vegetables. Cover two-thirds of the way up the leek with water and 2 tablespoons of the butter and bring to a simmer over medium heat. Cover and gently simmer for 30 to 40 minutes, or until tender. Remove from the pan and cool. Place the fennel juice in a small saucepan and, over medium heat, bring to a simmer, then strain through cheesecloth. Place the fennel juice back in the saucepan and simmer for 10 minutes, or until reduced by one-third. Chop half of the roasted fennel into a small dice and fold it into the brown basmati rice along with 3 tablespoons of the fennel fronds. Season to taste with salt and pepper. Place the remaining roasted fennel in a blender with the fennel juice and purée until smooth. Strain through a fine-mesh sieve and season to taste with salt and pepper. Warm just prior to use. Place the small-diced fennel in a small saucepan with the remaining 1 tablespoon butter and cook over medium heat for 4 to 5 minutes. Add the Red Wine Reduction and continue to cook for 3 to 4 minutes, or until most of the red wine has been absorbed by the fennel.

ASSEMBLY  Place a ring mold in the center of each plate and spoon in some of the hot rice mixture and remove the mold. Place some of the diced fennel on top and around the rice. Place 1 of the leek halves on top, and sprinkle with the remaining fennel fronds. Spoon the fennel purée around the mold and drizzle some of the white truffle oil around the purée.

## Wine Notes

Truffle aromas pervade the tabletop with this preparation, suggesting a heady wine. Oak aromas in white Burgundy are friendly with this dish, as is the richness of Chardonnay. No producer extrudes as much earthy character from ripe fruit as Michel Niellon, a magnificent Chassagne-Montrachet winemaker. A young example will burst with vibrant fruit, and a mature one with developed earthiness and almond overtones. These aromas and flavors match the nuttiness of the rice and the almost-caramelized flavor of the fennel and leeks.

# Rhubarb Napoleon with Preserved Ginger, Vanilla Mascarpone, and Rhubarb Sauce

~~~~~~~~~~~~~~~~~~~~~~~~~~~~~~~~~~~~~~~~~~~~~~~~~~~~~~~~~~~~~~~

*Braised rhubarb has to be one of my favorite desserts. Its flavor is clear and straightforward,*
*but sophisticated. I had a little fun with the presentation by layering the lightly cooked rhubarb with*
*vanilla-flavored mascarpone and crispy filo pieces to create a wonderfully textured napoleon.*
*Oven-dried rhubarb strips augment the rhubarb flavor and add a further textural element.*
*Finally, the mint syrup provides a touch of sweetness to counterbalance the slightly tart rhubarb sauce.*

**Serves 4**

*1½ cups granulated sugar*

*2 cups water*

*6 stalks rhubarb*

*6 sheets whole wheat filo*

*3 tablespoons butter, melted*

*2 tablespoons confectioners' sugar*

*1 cup fresh rhubarb juice*

*½ cup fresh strawberry juice*

*½ cup heavy cream*

*2 tablespoons julienned gingerroot*

*1 vanilla bean, split lengthwise with pulp scraped out and reserved*

*4 tablespoons mascarpone*

*2 tablespoons Preserved Ginger (see Appendices)*

*Mint Syrup (see Appendices)*

METHOD   Place 1 cup of the granulated sugar and the water in a medium saucepan. Simmer for 3 to 4 minutes, or until the sugar is dissolved. Cut 2 stalks of the rhubarb in half. Using a vegetable peeler, peel long, thick strips of rhubarb, the length of the stalk. Add the rhubarb strips to the saucepan and simmer for 2 minutes, or until they just begin to soften. Immediately remove from the saucepan and reserve the cooking liquid. Lay the strips flat on a nonstick sheet pan, making sure that they do not overlap. Bake at 250 degrees for 20 to 30 minutes, or until they are lightly golden and appear dry to the touch; watch them carefully, as they can burn very quickly. Shortly after removing them from the oven, loosen them from the pan; they should become crisp. Lay flat 1 sheet of whole wheat filo on a work surface. Brush with the melted butter and sprinkle lightly with granulated sugar. Lay another piece of filo on top and repeat with the melted butter and the sugar. Top with 1 more piece of filo and set aside. Repeat this process to complete another set of 3 layers. Cut eight 2-inch squares from both sets of the filo sheets, for a total of 16 squares. Place a piece of parchment paper on a sheet pan. Lay the filo squares on the parchment paper and cover with another piece of parchment and a sheet pan. Bake at 350 degrees for 10 to 12 minutes, or until golden brown. Sprinkle the top of the filo squares with confectioners' sugar and, using a blow torch, gently caramelize the sugar; watch closely so they do not burn.

Place the rhubarb and strawberry juices in a small saucepan with ¼ cup of the granulated sugar. Bring to a simmer and reduce for 20 to 30 minutes, or until you have about ½ cup of juice. Strain through a fine-mesh sieve covered with 3 layers of cheesecloth. In a small saucepan, place the heavy cream and ginger. Bring to a simmer and let sit for 15 minutes, then strain and cool. Place the cool cream in a small mixing bowl with the pulp from the vanilla bean. Using a whisk, whip until soft peaks begin to form, add 2 tablespoons of the granulated sugar, and continue to whip until firm. Add the mascarpone and whip until incorporated. Refrigerate until ready to use.

Cut the remaining rhubarb into ½-inch pieces on the bias. Place the cooking liquid from the rhubarb strips in a medium sauté pan. Add the rhubarb and bring to a simmer. Continue to cook for about 3 to 5 minutes, or until the rhubarb is tender.

ASSEMBLY   Place a teaspoon of the mascarpone cream, 2 pieces of the rhubarb, and a piece of the julienned ginger in the center of each plate. Place a filo square on top and layer with the mascarpone cream, rhubarb, and Preserved Ginger. Continue until you have 4 layers of the napoleon. Top the final layer with some of the mascarpone cream and a piece of rhubarb. Lay a piece of ginger at the base of each side of the napoleon and, using this as your anchor, lay a strip of the dried rhubarb against each side, pointing upright. Spoon some of the rhubarb sauce, Mint Syrup, and a dash of the Preserved Ginger syrup around the napoleon.

## Wine Notes

Mint adds a refreshing counterpoint to the sweet and spicy napoleon, so a sweet wine with a slight green streak could be a great match: the Pinot Gris *Selection de Grains Nobles* from the Heimbourg vineyard by Zind Humbrecht 1991 provides an amazing synthesis of rhubarb, ginger, mint, and strawberry flavors. The Austrian Kracher Scheurebe Beerenauslese, also a 1991, comes close to the intensity of the *Selection de Grains Nobles* but is just a tad peppery. Both of these rare wines are, unfortunately, pricey and hard to find, but they are perfect for this dessert.

*Sing, voice of Spring, till I too blossom and rejoice and sing.*

CHRISTINA ROSSETTI

May is one of my favorite months because it bridges spring and summer. The clean air and sparkling sun are refreshing signs that beautiful and varied foodstuffs now abound. It's time for sweet Vidalia onions, ultra-earthy fiddlehead ferns, sweet snow peas, crunchy yellow wax beans, and several types of crispy radishes. Sharp watercress and peppery arugula once again provide a discernable contrast to the succulent fruits like French melons and persimmons. Sweet bell peppers also populate the markets, as does the lovely elephant garlic. For the adventuresome, braised cattails beckon. ⅄ Until May evenings turn warm, the body yearns for something filling. Whole wheat couscous or Adzuki beans may be perfect. Flavoring agents such as lovage, lemongrass, and horseradish are each strong enough to punctuate meals on cool evenings, but delicate enough for warm fragrant nights. Finally, in May, delicious stone fruits become available. The apricot—sweet, luscious, and tart—is a marvelous end to a late spring feast.

# Brown Turkey Figs, French Melon, and Persimmon with Arugula, Wild Watercress, and Black Pepper—Vanilla Bean Vinaigrette

*This salad could either be served assembled, as it is presented here, or simply tossed together for a more rustic presentation. The key to this dish is the vinaigrette. The spicy, perfumed black pepper—vanilla bean vinaigrette brings the sweet fruits and the sharp, astringent lettuces perfectly into balance. Other fruits or lettuces could be substituted for a more than satisfactory result.*

**Serves 4**

*2 teaspoons rice vinegar*

*2 teaspoons lime juice*

*1/2 cup olive oil*

*1 tablespoon cracked black pepper*

*1 vanilla bean, split lengthwise with pulp scraped out and reserved*

*Salt and pepper*

*2 brown turkey figs*

*2 persimmons*

*1 French melon*

*2 cups arugula*

*2 cups wild watercress*

*1 tablespoon purple geranium petals*

METHOD Place the rice vinegar and lime juice in a small bowl. Slowly whisk in the olive oil and add the black pepper and vanilla pulp. Season to taste with salt and pepper.

Cut each fig into 6 wedges and set aside. Peel the persimmons and cut each into 6 wedges; remove the seeds. Cut the melon in half and remove the seeds and peel. Slice the melon into 16 thin slices. Place the arugula and watercress in a medium bowl, gently toss with 3 tablespoons of the vinaigrette, and season to taste with salt and pepper.

ASSEMBLY Place some of the greens in the center of each plate. Place 3 wedges each of the figs and persimmons, and 4 slices of the melon at separate points (to form a rough triangle). Sprinkle each plate with the geraniums, and spoon some of the remaining vinaigrette around the plate.

### Wine Notes

This refreshing fruit and bitter green salad needs a very light, refreshing wine. A Moscato d'Asti is ideal with its low alcohol and peachy sweet fruit, or a light, extremely fresh Viognier, like the spring-released Rabbit Ridge *Heartbreak Hill*, gives more weight and less sugar, but can be equally refreshing. Be careful with the black pepper here, especially if the dish is served with a Viognier—the heat could be overemphasized.

# Roasted Whole Vidalia Onions with Whole Wheat Couscous and Veal Stock Reduction

~~~~~~~~~~~~~~~~~~~~~~~~~~~~~~~~~~~~~~~~~~~~~~~~~~~~~~~~~~~~

*There is nothing quite like eating a succulent, whole roasted Vidalia onion.*
*It is already quite sweet in its raw form, but when roasted its natural sugars begin to caramelize*
*and it is almost like eating a piece of vegetable candy. In this preparation*
*I have added asparagus tips, yellow wax beans, and whole wheat couscous along*
*with some Veal Stock Reduction to create a substantial entrée.*
*Pea blossoms folded into the couscous at the last moment add an exotically elegant flavor*
*that helps tame the rich overtones of this combination of ingredients.*

**Serves 4**

*4 Vidalia onions, peeled*

*Salt and pepper*

*³/₄ cup yellow wax beans (about 3 ounces), cleaned and blanched*

*³/₄ cup purple asparagus (about 3 ounces), blanched*

*3 cups cooked whole wheat couscous*

*³/₄ cup snow peas (about 3 ounces), cleaned and blanched*

*2 tablespoons olive oil*

*¹/₂ cup Veal Stock Reduction (see Appendices)*

*1 tablespoon butter*

*2 tablespoons pea blossoms*

METHOD  Place the onions in a ovenproof pan, cover halfway with water, and bake at 375 degrees for 1¹/₂ hours. Turn the onions upside down, place back into the oven, and continue to cook for an additional 1¹/₂ hours, or until extremely tender. Remove from the liquid and cool completely. Once cool, remove and discard the outer layer of the onion. Using your finger, gently remove the inner rings of the onion, leaving the two outer layers intact. Place the inner portion of the onion in a blender and purée until smooth. Pass through a fine-mesh sieve and season to taste with salt and pepper.

Cut half of the yellow wax beans into quarters on the bias. Cut the asparagus into 2-inch julienne. Fold the quartered beans into the couscous along with half of the asparagus and the snow peas. Fill each onion with some of the couscous mixture, spoon the olive oil along the outside of the onion, and bake at 350 degrees for 4 to 5 minutes, or until hot. Place the onion purée and the Veal Stock Reduction in separate small saucepans and warm over medium heat. Sauté the remaining asparagus and snow peas in 1 tablespoon of butter over medium heat for 2 minutes, or until hot.

ASSEMBLY  Spoon some of the roasted onion purée in the center of each plate. Place some of the hot vegetables in the center of the purée and place the whole onion mouth up on top of the vegetables. Place a few pea blossoms on top of the onion and spoon some of the Veal Stock Reduction and additional onion purée around the plate.

## Wine Notes

With its light meat reduction and sweet, earthy flavors, this preparation seems to lean slightly in the direction of red wine. The sweet Vidalia onion needs some of the rooty echoes that red Burgundy provides. A delicate Burgundy from a soft, forward vintage will be the most pleasant option here. One of the softer Crus of the house of Joseph Drouhin such as Chambolle-Musigny or a Beaune from 1992 are elegant matches, as is our favorite Chambolle producer in the lighter style, Domaine Bertheau. If the recipe is altered to exclude the Veal Stock Reduction, a fairly heavily oaked (read sweetly caramelized) Chardonnay is effective; Sarah's Vineyard *Lot II* has enough weight and wood for the lightly sweet couscous and the richly sweet caramelized onion purée.

# Ragout of Fiddlehead Ferns, White Carrots, and Adzuki and Lima Beans with French Morning and Icicle Radishes

*Fiddlehead ferns have a complex yet lean flavor. That is why I like to pair them
with something fat and rich like braised legumes. This dish perfectly exemplifies this idea,
but then takes it a step further by incorporating "lean" icicle radishes and "fat, rich" white carrots.
The flavors and textures in the idea of "lean and fat" are unanimously extolled in this ragout,
and the bean juices seem to tie everything together.*

**Serves 4**

*¹/₂ cup fresh adzuki beans*

*¹/₂ cup fresh speckled lima beans*

*4 tablespoons butter*

*8 red icicle radishes, sliced in half
lengthwise*

*6 French morning radishes,
sliced in half lengthwise*

*Salt and pepper*

*12 white carrots, peeled and roasted*

*3 tablespoons chopped parsley, chives,
or other fresh herbs*

*2 cups fiddlehead ferns, cleaned
and blanched*

METHOD Place the fresh beans in 2 separate small saucepans, cover with water, and add 1 tablespoon of butter to each saucepan. Simmer over medium heat for 10 to 15 minutes, or until tender. Drain the beans and reserve the cooking liquid.

Place the radishes in a medium sauté pan with the cut side down, add 2 teaspoons of the butter, and sauté over medium heat for 4 to 5 minutes, or until slightly golden and tender. Season to taste with salt and pepper. Place the carrots on a sheet pan with 1 teaspoon butter. Bake at 375 degrees for 15 minutes, or until tender, turning the carrots once for even cooking. Place the bean cooking liquid in a small saucepan and simmer over medium heat for 3 to 5 minutes, or until reduced to ¹/₂ cup. Whisk in 2 teaspoons of the butter and the chopped herbs. Blanch the fiddlehead ferns in boiling salted water, toss with the remaining 1 teaspoon butter, and season to taste with salt and pepper.

ASSEMBLY Place some of the fiddlehead ferns, radishes, white carrots, adzuki beans, and lima beans in the center of each plate. Spoon some of the bean reduction–herb sauce around the plate.

**Wine Notes**

Fiddlehead ferns can be as difficult as asparagus or green beans to match properly with wine, but the adzuki beans present enough creamy texture to "fatten" the dish and allow an aromatic dry white wine to add flavor. A clean Viognier, such as the Alban Estate from San Luis Obispo, California, emphasizes freshness and lightness while delivering great independent flavor, and a dry Rosé, such as Domaine Tempier Bandol Rosé, underscores the sweet white carrot flavor while balancing the rest of the elements.

# Vegetable Pavé with Lemon Thyme—Infused Vegetable Broth

*This Mediterranean vegetable pavé can be served like a pasta-free lasagne.
Or if you desire a more substantial dish, lasagne noodles could easily be added.
In either case, the preparation is fairly straightforward and quite light.
The broth is both delicate and full-flavored, especially with the infusion of lemon thyme.
Perhaps best of all, both the pavé and the broth can be made well in advance and
the portion size can be adjusted according to the needs of your menu.*

**Serves 4**

*2 tablespoons butter*

*1 Idaho potato, peeled and sliced lengthwise
into thin slices*

*Salt and pepper*

*½ cup grated Parmesan*

*2 red bell peppers, roasted and cleaned*

*2 yellow bell peppers, roasted and cleaned*

*1 yellow squash, sliced lengthwise in
¼-inch-thick slices*

*6 artichoke bottoms and stems, cooked and
cut into thin slices*

*1 zucchini, sliced lengthwise in
¼-inch-thick slices*

*6 cups Blond Vegetable Stock
(see Appendices)*

*4 fresh sprigs lemon thyme*

METHOD  Line a 4 by 4-inch baking pan
with aluminum foil. Grease the foil with 1
tablespoon of the butter. Using one third of
the potatoes, form a layer of slices, with the
potatoes slightly overlapping each other.
Lightly season each layer with salt and
pepper and sprinkle with some of the
Parmesan. Cut the bell peppers into wide
slices. Place a layer of the red bell pepper
on top of the potato, followed by layers of
yellow squash, artichokes, yellow bell pepper, and zucchini. Repeat with another
layer of potato and all of the vegetables.
Finally, end with one last layer of potato.
Cover with aluminum foil and bake at 375
degrees for 2 hours with a weighted pan set
on top of the dish. (This will keep it packed
tightly during the cooking and cooling
processes). Meanwhile, place the Blond
Vegetable Stock in a medium saucepan and
reduce to 4 cups. Add the lemon thyme and
simmer for 10 minutes. Strain, reserving
the thyme, and season to taste with salt and
pepper. Remove the pavé from the oven and
allow it to cool in the refrigerator with the
weighted pan on top. Once cool, remove it
from the pan and cut into four 2-inch
squares. Place the squares in a nonstick pan
with the remaining tablespoon butter.
Sauté over medium heat until both sides
are golden brown.

ASSEMBLY  Place a piece of the pavé in the
center of each bowl. Ladle some of the
Blond Vegetable Stock in each bowl. Garnish with the springs of lemon thyme.

## Wine Notes

These vegetable flavors require firmness
yet aromatic delicacy in the wine accompaniment. We find that Châteauneuf-du-
Pape Blanc is most useful. The firm, dry
Château La Nerthe Blanc is best, with a
fine crisp finish that matches the lemon
thyme influence and bell pepper sweetness.
The full-bodied, but not oaky, core of this
wine seems well tuned to the potato that
structures the presentation of the dish.

# Elephant Garlic Soup with Cattails and Lovage

~~~~~~~~~~~~~~~~~~~~~~~~~~~~~~~~~~~~~~~~~~~~~~~~~~~~~~~~~~~~~~~~~~~~~~~~~~~~~~~~~~~~~~~~~~~~~~~~~~~~~~~~~~~~~~~~~

*Garlic poached in milk is so sweet and luscious—it truly is delightful. This is especially true
with elephant garlic, which seems to be all the more creamy and delicate. Although this soup is made
without cream, it very much has the texture and feel of a cream-based preparation.
I have added exotic but delicious braised cattails to this simply prepared soup and the result is a beautifully
satisfying combination of flavors. A little lovage and some chives add the only necessary accent.*

### Serves 4

3 heads elephant garlic, peeled

10 cups of milk

1/2 cup olive oil

2 cups Blond Vegetable Stock
(see Appendices)

Salt and pepper

1 cup cattails, thoroughly cleaned

2 tablespoons butter

1 tablespoon chopped chives

2 tablespoons lovage, cut into
fine chiffonade

METHOD Place the garlic in a medium saucepan with 3 cups of the milk. Simmer for 5 minutes over medium heat, then strain, discarding the milk. Repeat this process two more times. Place the garlic in an ovenproof pan with the olive oil, cover, and bake at 350 degrees for 40 minutes. Remove the garlic from the pan, reserving the oil, and place in a blender with the remaining 1 cup milk and the Blond Vegetable Stock. Purée until smooth, strain through a fine-mesh sieve, and season to taste with salt and pepper. Place the cleaned cattails in boiling salted water for 5 minutes, then shock in ice water. Place the cattails in a small saucepan with the butter and cover with water. Simmer over medium heat for 30 to 40 minutes, or until tender. Remove from the liquid and season to taste with salt and pepper. Lightly toss the cattails with the chives and 1 tablespoon of the olive oil that was cooked with the garlic. Season to taste with salt and pepper.

ASSEMBLY Ladle some of the hot soup into each bowl. Place a few of the cattails on top of the soup and sprinkle some of the lovage around the bowl. Top with freshly ground pepper.

### Wine Notes

The elephant garlic is rich and sweet, rather than pungent, and needs a wine with the same attributes. Most Chardonnays will be too heavy and smoky. The more aromatic varieties (Riesling, Viognier, Marsanne, Gewürztraminer) fail with garlic prepared in this style. Oregon Pinot Gris with a touch of oak is practical. The Au Bon Climat Aligote also meshes well with these flavors.

# Baby Red and Green Romaine
## with Horseradish Caesar Dressing
## and One-Eyed Susans

*This version of a Caesar salad could be an elegant start to a more formal dinner.*
*I have used horseradish in lieu of anchovies in the dressing and the result is something that is less*
*musty, and pungent, but a little more tangy. The "one-eyed Susan" gives you both*
*the crouton and egg element in one shot. Small spring onions add the perfect zing and crunch,*
*while the baby lettuces are so buttery and soft that they just melt into the dressing.*

**Serves 4**

*1 egg yolk*

*1 tablespoon rice vinegar*

*1/2 cup olive oil*

*1/3 cup grated horseradish*

*2 tablespoons grated Parmesan*

*Salt and pepper*

*8 slices Brioche (recipe follows),*
*sliced 1/2 inch thick*

*1 teaspoon butter*

*8 quail eggs*

*12 leaves baby red romaine*

*12 leaves baby green romaine*

*1/4 cup thinly sliced purple spring onion*

*2 tablespoons Parmesan flakes*

METHOD Place the egg yolk and vinegar in a small bowl and slowly whisk in 6 tablespoons of the olive oil. Add the horseradish and Parmesan and season to taste with salt and pepper.

Cut eight 1¾-inch circles out of the Brioche slices, then cut a 1-inch circle out of the center of each circle. Place the butter in a medium nonstick pan and sauté the Brioche circles for 1 minute over medium heat, until golden brown on one side. Turn over, crack open a quail egg, and place it in the center of each circle. Continue to cook over medium-low heat for 3 to 4 minutes, or until the egg is just cooked. Place the red and green romaine in a medium bowl and toss with the remaining 2 tablespoons olive oil. Season to taste with salt and pepper.

ASSEMBLY Place 3 red and 3 green romaine leaves in the center of each plate. Place 2 of the Brioche–quail egg circles on top of the leaves. Place some of the purple spring onions on top of the romaine and spoon some of the horseradish dressing across the leaves. Top with freshly ground pepper.

## Brioche

*1 tablespoon active dry yeast*

*1/4 cup sugar*

*4 tablespoons warm water*

*6 eggs*

*1 tablespoon kosher salt*

*4 cups flour*

*2 cups butter, softened*

METHOD In a medium bowl, dissolve the yeast and 2 tablespoons of the sugar in the warm water. In another bowl, beat the eggs with the remaining 2 tablespoons sugar and the salt. Sift the flour onto a table and make a well in the center. Pour the yeast and the eggs into the well. Using your fingertips, mix until well combined. The dough will be moist and sticky. Knead for several minutes. Cut in the butter. Place the dough in an oiled bowl and cover with plastic wrap. Punch down after dough has doubled in size (about 1 to 2 hours). Place into 2 buttered and floured bread pans and cover with plastic wrap. Let sit for 1 hour, then bake at 375 degrees for 30 to 40 minutes, or until golden brown. Remove from the pans and cool on a wire rack.

## Wine Notes

This "thinking man's" Caesar salad is well balanced by Champagne, and especially a leesy, yeasty one. Horseradish and sparkling wine merge beautifully, and the brioche and onion elements beg for a Chardonnay-based sparkler. Try a small grower-producer like Batiste-Pertois, Egly-Ouriet, or J. Lassalle in a Blanc de Blancs style.

# Apricot Basmati Rice Pudding with Apricot Juice and Lemongrass Anglaise

*Basmati is wonderful for rice pudding because it is a little chewier than ordinary rice and thus renders something with more texture. Paired with apricots and Lemongrass Anglaise, the three marvelous flavors work in perfect harmony. The lacy tuiles, or Brandy Snaps, add an important textural component, while the wild Hawaiian ginger incorporates the perfect exotic element.*

**Serves 4**

*½ cup white basmati rice*

*1 cup milk*

*¼ cup water*

*½ cup plus 3 tablespoons sugar*

*3 (2-inch-long) pieces of lemongrass*

*2 cups apricot juice*

*8 small apricots, peeled*

*2 tablespoons chopped Hawaiian ginger*

*8 Brandy Snaps (recipe follows)*

*Lemongrass Anglaise (recipe follows)*

METHOD Place the rice in a small saucepan with the milk, water, ½ cup of the sugar, and the lemongrass. Simmer over low heat for 20 to 30 minutes. You may need to add some water if the milk is absorbed before the rice is cooked. Remove and discard the lemongrass and set aside at room temperature.

Place the apricot juice in a small saucepan and reduce over medium heat for 30 minutes, or until reduced to ⅓ cup. Strain through a fine-mesh sieve and set aside. Cut 4 apricots into small dice and sauté over medium heat for 3 minutes with 2 tablespoons of the sugar and the Hawaiian ginger. Cut the remaining 4 apricots into thin slices.

ASSEMBLY Place one Brandy Snap in the center of each plate. Place a small ring mold on top of the Brandy Snap and fill with a layer of rice. Top with some of the diced apricot and place another Brandy Snap on top of the apricot. Spread another layer of rice over the Brandy Snap and arrange the sliced apricots in a pinwheel on top of the rice. Sprinkle the apricots with 1 tablespoon of the sugar and lightly caramelize the sugar with a blowtorch. Remove the mold. Spoon the Lemongrass Anglaise and apricot reduction around the plate.

## Brandy Snaps

Yield: 8

*2 tablespoons butter, softened*

*¼ cup confectioners' sugar*

*2 tablespoons honey*

*2 tablespoons brandy*

*⅓ cup flour*

*Pinch of salt*

METHOD Place the butter and sugar in a small bowl. Combine with a fork, add the honey and brandy, and stir until smooth. Add the flour and salt and stir until smooth. Place 8 rounded teaspoons of batter on a nonstick sheet pan about 2 inches apart, and spread into 1½-inch circles. Place in the oven at 350 degrees for 3 to 5 minutes, or until golden brown. Once slightly cool, remove from the pan.

## Lemongrass Anglaise

Yield: 1 cup

*2 egg yolks*

*4 teaspoons sugar*

*1 cup heavy cream*

*¼ cup chopped lemongrass*

METHOD In a bowl, whisk together the yolks and sugar until smooth. Place the heavy cream and lemongrass in a small saucepan and bring to a boil over medium heat. Temper the yolks with the hot cream while whipping constantly. Return the mixture to the saucepan and cook over medium heat, stirring constantly, for 2 minutes, or until it coats the back of a spoon. Do not boil the mixture. Strain through a fine-mesh sieve and cool.

## Wine Notes

The most "apricotty" wine in our repertoire would be a vibrant dessert style Muscat. Two stand out in tasting: Muskat Ottonel Beerenauslese by the brilliant Alois Kracher of Austria, and the *Alpianae* by Vignalta of the Veneto. These are at once richer and earthier than the American sweet Muscats, and because of firm acidity, can stand up to the intensity of the lemongrass.

I am unabashedly elated when the first days of summer arrive. This is when I get to work with some of the year's most alluring produce while I can still enjoy a full meal—before the summer heat seeps in and makes many dishes seem burdensome. ꩜ To me, June is synonymous with exuberance, mostly because the flavors and colors of the month's offering are so dramatic. Sugar snap peas are sweet and abundant, and velvety avocados, prickly artichokes, and hauntingly fragrant porcini mushrooms inspire endless combinations. Haricots verts are tender and supple. Fresh black-eyed peas, a special treat, demand attention. Delicate pea shoots are refreshing and add a refined complexity to any dish. And the unusual loquat lends an exotic touch to desserts. I like elegant, playful spicing in June, which is perfect for these fresh ingredients. I'm not yet ready for the big, assertive spices and flavors of late summer.

# Chilled Sugar Snap Pea and
# Mint Soup with Avocado

*The first peas of the summer are sweet and exploding with flavor.*
*Although they work brilliantly in a number of preparations, I particularly favor them*
*in this chilled soup. It is very simple to make and is quite refreshing*
*for the first hot days of the season. The addition of mint and pink peppercorns is*
*just enough of an exotic accent, and the avocado lends a delicate richness.*
*Finally, the tomato adds just the right amount of sweet acid to tie all of the flavors together.*

**Serves 4**

*2 cups shelled sugar snap peas, blanched*

*2¹/₂ cups sugar snap pea shells, blanched*

*¹/₃ cup blanched fresh mint leaves*

*¹/₂ cup plus 1 tablespoon water*

*Salt and pepper*

*6 teaspoons olive oil*

*2 tablespoons minced shallots*

*1 cup tomato concassée*

*2 tablespoons crème fraîche*

*1 tablespoon pink peppercorns, roasted and coarsely ground*

*1 avocado, peeled and diced*

*1 tablespoon freshly squeezed lime juice*

*4 small sprigs mint*

METHOD Place 1 cup of the peas, the pea shells, blanched mint, and ¹/₂ cup of the water in a blender. Purée until smooth. Strain through a fine-mesh sieve and season to taste with salt and pepper.

Place 2 teaspoons of the olive oil and the shallots in a medium sauté pan. Sweat until translucent, then add the tomato concassée. Continue to cook for 4 to 5 minutes, until most of the tomato juice has been reduced. Remove from the pan and cool. In a small bowl, combine the remaining 1 tablespoon of water, crème fraîche, and pink peppercorns and season to taste with salt. Toss the avocado with the lime juice and season to taste with salt and pepper.

ASSEMBLY Place some of the avocado in the center of each bowl and top with the tomato mixture. (You may use a ring mold or a small timbale if a more structured presentation is desired.) Place the remaining 1 cup peas around the avocado and ladle in some of the soup. Drizzle the crème fraîche mixture and the remaining 4 teaspoons olive oil over the soup. Place a few mint leaves on top of the tomato mixture.

## Wine Notes

Here the intensity of the mint drives the soup, with creamy avocado richness soothing the palate. The wine choice should allow the pea sweetness to shine amidst these more dominant flavors. An aromatic, oakless Pinot Blanc makes the best match—Gustave Lorentz, a fine Alsatian producer, makes a good one. In a drier style with more piercing acidity, Puiatti Pinot Bianco is very successful. You may find that Sauvignon Blanc is too dry and astringent; Viognier is too heady and perfumed.

# Black-Eyed Peas with Haricots Verts and Spicy Curry Emulsion

*Fresh black-eyed peas are a fantastic treat and they are far superior in flavor and texture to their dried counterparts. Here they are combined with haricots verts, pea shoots, and a very flavorful curry emulsion sauce. This preparation works well as an appetizer, or place slices of poached chicken on top for a more substantial dish.*

**Serves 4**

*1½ cups fresh black-eyed peas*

*4 cloves garlic*

*7 tablespoons plus 2 teaspoons butter*

*½ cup Blond Vegetable Stock (see Appendices)*

*3 tablespoons freshly squeezed orange juice*

*⅛ teaspoon cayenne*

*¼ teaspoon paprika*

*½ teaspoon curry powder*

*¼ teaspoon togarashi*

*2 teaspoons turmeric*

*Salt and pepper*

*2 cups haricots verts, blanched*

*2 tablespoons chopped parsley, chives, or other fresh herbs*

*4 whole chives, blanched*

*2 cups pea shoots*

*2 tablespoons water*

*2 teaspoons black sesame seeds, toasted*

METHOD Place the black-eyed peas in a medium saucepan with the garlic and 2 tablespoons of the butter, and cover with water. Bring to a simmer and slowly cook for 20 to 30 minutes, or until the peas are tender. Remove the garlic cloves from the pan and cut into quarters. Place the vegetable stock, orange juice, cayenne, paprika, curry powder, togarashi, and turmeric in a small saucepan. Bring to a simmer, whisk in 4 tablespoons of the butter, and season to taste with salt and pepper. Before serving, froth the sauce with a hand blender for 3 minutes, or until thick.

Heat the haricots verts in 2 teaspoons of the butter in a medium sauté pan. Season to taste with salt and pepper and toss with the chopped herbs and 1 more teaspoon butter. Divide the haricots verts into 4 bundles, tie with a chive, and set aside. Place the pea shoots in a medium sauté pan with the remaining 2 teaspoons butter and the water. Gently wilt the pea shoots in the sauté pan over medium heat for 1 minute. Season to taste with salt and pepper.

ASSEMBLY Place a mound of the black-eyed peas in the center of each plate and scatter the garlic around the plate. Set a bundle of haricots verts on top of the peas and place some of the wilted pea shoots around the plate. Spoon the frothed spicy curry sauce on top of the peas and sprinkle some of the toasted black sesame seeds around the plate.

**Wine Notes**

This dish emphasizes the peppery flavors of the sauce more than the soothing creaminess of the legumes. A wine of modest alcohol will tend to refresh while mitigating the hot elements. A favorite Rheingau style, the Schloss Reichartshausen Riesling Halbtrocken, has the appropriate sweetness level but seems a bit rich even at only 11.5 percent alcohol. A classic Mosel at closer to 8 percent is more refreshing. We imagine a Graacher from Dr. Loosen or Willi Schaefer.

# Grilled Porcini Mushrooms with Tomato Water, Roasted Soybeans, and Sesame Oil

*This preparation really emphasizes the beautiful earthiness and meatiness of the mushrooms. The slow grilling and the sesame flavor add a subtle exotic accent to the rich and profound flavor of the porcini. The Tomato Water acts as the contrasting backdrop and further highlights the haunting characteristics of the mushrooms. The soybean and glasswort add textural and flavor accents that help give this simple preparation considerable depth. Shiitake, oyster, or even button mushrooms could be substituted with more than excellent results.*

**Serves 4**

*32 (2-inch) wedges of porcini mushrooms (about 4 cups)*

*½ cup sesame oil*

*Salt and pepper*

*8 rosemary skewers, soaked in water for 3 hours*

*1 cup glasswort, blanched*

*4 cups Tomato Water (see Appendices)*

*½ cup Roasted Soybeans (recipe follows)*

METHOD Toss the mushrooms in 6 tablespoons of the sesame oil and season lightly with salt and pepper. Thread 4 mushroom wedges on each rosemary skewer. Place the skewers on the grill over a moderate flame and grill until the mushrooms are tender, about 10 minutes. In a saucepan, reheat the glasswort in a few tablespoons of Tomato Water over medium heat for 2 to 3 minutes. Place the remaining Tomato Water in a separate small saucepan and warm until hot over medium heat. Season to taste with salt and pepper.

ASSEMBLY Place some of the glasswort and Roasted Soybeans in the center of each bowl. Place 2 of the mushroom skewers on top of the glasswort. Ladle some of the Tomato Water in each bowl and spoon the remaining sesame oil around the rim of the bowl.

## Roasted Soybeans

Yield: about ½ cup

*½ cup uncooked golden soybeans*

*2 tablespoons olive oil*

*Salt*

METHOD Soak the soybeans in water overnight. Drain, place on a sheet pan, and toss with olive oil and salt. Place in the oven at 350 degrees for 20 minutes, stirring every 5 minutes to ensure even cooking. The beans should be golden brown and crunchy. Season to taste with salt and store in a tightly covered container until needed.

### Wine Notes

The flavors of Hidalgo's *La Gitana* Manzanilla Sherry, with its characteristic seaside tanginess, marry well with the beans and Tomato Water. With this preparation served as a middle course, though, an apéritif wine such as this is probably not as appropriate as a dry table wine. Both red and white can be useful: the dry Chenin Blanc of Chalone provides enough body for the mushroom and soy flavors and enough acidity for the Tomato Water, and the freshly fruity Pinot Noir of Robert Sinskey, a fine Carneros grower, is not as overwhelming as other reds might be, providing a complementary ripe fruitiness for the earthy, slightly salty effect of the dish.

# Barley "Risotto" with Herb Juice, Artichoke Chips, and Veal Stock Reduction

*In this dish I cook the barley just like one would cook arborio rice for a risotto,
by adding the liquid little by little and carefully stirring throughout the cooking process.
The result is a soft and creamy but still al dente texture. Cooked artichoke pieces are
folded into the barley at the last moment to add a nice meaty contrast to the grain. Artichoke
chips are introduced to not only emphasize the artichoke flavor but also to add an
important textural element. The Parmesan flakes add a pleasant richness, and the meat juice
helps all the flavors realize their complexity with its elegant fullness.*

**Serves 4**

*2 shallots, minced*

*2 cloves garlic, minced*

*4 tablespoons butter*

*1 cup raw barley, toasted*

*4 to 5 cups Vegetable Stock (see Appendices)*

*Salt and pepper*

*2 raw artichoke hearts, choke removed and thinly sliced*

*2 cups plus 1 tablespoon grapeseed oil*

*3 artichoke hearts, cooked and cut into small wedges*

*2 cups enoki mushrooms, cleaned*

*1/2 cup Herb Juice (recipe follows)*

*4 tablespoons Parmesan flakes*

*2 teaspoons marjoram blossoms*

*1/4 cup Veal Stock Reduction (see Appendices)*

METHOD Sweat the shallots and garlic with 2 tablespoons of the butter in a medium saucepan. Add the barley and 1 cup of the Vegetable Stock and continue to cook over medium heat while stirring occasionally until most of the liquid is absorbed. Continue to add the Vegetable Stock 1 cup at a time until the barley is thoroughly cooked. Season the cooked barley to taste with salt and pepper.

Fry the thinly sliced artichoke pieces in 2 cups of the grapeseed oil until golden brown. Transfer to paper towels and season with salt. Lightly caramelize the artichoke wedges with 1 tablespoon of the butter in a medium sauté pan and fold into the cooked barley. Quickly sauté the enoki mushrooms with the remaining 1 tablespoon butter over medium heat until tender, and season to taste with salt and pepper. Just before serving, fold the Herb Juice into the cooked barley.

ASSEMBLY Place some of the barley mixture in the center of each plate (you may use a ring mold for a neater presentation) and layer some of the artichoke chips and Parmesan flakes. Place the enoki mushrooms around the barley at four separate points. Sprinkle with the marjoram blossoms and spoon the Veal Stock Reduction around the plate.

## Herb Juice

Yield: about 3/4 cup

*1/4 cup olive oil*

*1 cup flat-leaf parsley*

*1/2 cup chives*

*1/2 cup basil*

*1/4 cup water*

*Salt and pepper*

METHOD Place 1 tablespoon of the olive oil and the herbs in a hot sauté pan and quickly sauté (30 to 45 seconds). Immediately remove the herbs from the pan and cool in the refrigerator. Coarsely chop the cooled herbs and place in the blender with the remaining olive oil and the water. Purée until smooth and pass through a fine-mesh sieve. Season to taste with salt and pepper.

## Wine Notes

The artichoke as prepared in this dish presents no insurmountable obstacle to matching wine as it often does; the dominant flavors to work with are the nuttiness of the barley and the richness of the meat juices. Rich, somewhat oaky wines are the most effective. The concentration and ripeness of Alban Roussanne, the rare Rhône grape grown successfully in a few California plantings, adds a fine richness and robust finish without the apparent sweetness of oaky Viognier, Pinot Blanc, or many Chardonnays. This logic extends to the rare Château de Beaucastel *Vieilles Vignes* Roussanne 1988 from Châteauneuf-du-Pape, a rich wine that improves with age and performs brilliantly here. Mature, patiently guarded Chardonnay can be useful too. The unusual Blackwood Canyon 1988 from Washington, a late release, has a smokiness one would expect from mature Burgundy; it is atypical and works very well with the dish.

# Crispy Potato Tuiles with Parsley Root, Pickled Golden Beets, Spaghetti Squash, and Opal Basil

*You don't see parsley root used too often, which is strange because it really is delicious and simple to work with. Here it is braised and layered with spaghetti squash, crispy potato tuiles, and some pieces of lightly pickled golden beets. Not only is it loaded with flavor and full of texture, but this dish is also quite light, making it perfect for an appetizer.*

**Serves 4**

*1 Idaho potato (about 10 ounces), baked and peeled*

*4 tablespoons butter*

*4 egg whites*

*2 tablespoons chopped parsley, chives, or other fresh herbs*

*Salt and pepper*

*12 baby golden beets*

*1 cup Pickling Juice (see Appendices)*

*6 parsley roots, peeled*

*1/4 cup plus 5 tablespoons water*

*3 tablespoons freshly squeezed lemon juice*

*1/2 cup spaghetti squash, cooked*

*1/4 cup opal basil, cut into fine chiffonade*

*2 tablespoons Basil Oil (see Appendices)*

METHOD Place the warm potato in a mixing bowl with 2 tablespoons of the butter and the egg whites. Using an electric mixer fitted with the paddle attachment, mix on medium for 3 to 4 minutes, or until smooth. Pass the potato mixture through a fine-mesh sieve, fold in the chopped herbs, and season to taste with salt and pepper. Cut a 2-inch-square template out of a thin piece of cardboard. Place the template on a nonstick sheet pan, spread a thin layer of the potato batter in the center of the template, and remove the template. Repeat until you have 16 squares of batter. Place the sheet pan in the oven at 350 degrees for 7 to 10 minutes, or until the batter is golden brown. Remove the squares from the sheet pan and let cool.

Place the golden beets in a small saucepan and cover with water. Bring to a simmer over medium heat and cook for 15 minutes, or until the skin can be easily removed from the beets. Place 8 of the peeled beets in the Pickling Juice and let sit for 2 hours in the refrigerator. Remove from the Pickling Juice and cut into quarters. Place the remaining 4 beets in a blender with 3 to 5 tablespoons of the water and purée until smooth. Pass through a fine-mesh sieve and season to taste with salt and pepper. Place the purée into a small saucepan and, over medium heat, whisk in 1 tablespoon of the butter. Set aside and warm just prior to use.

Slice the parsley root into 1/4-inch slices on the bias. Place in a sauté pan with the remaining 1 tablespoon butter, 1/4 cup water, and 1 tablespoon of the lemon juice. Over medium heat, cook for 4 to 5 minutes, or until tender. Remove from the pan, toss with 1 tablespoon of the lemon juice, and season to taste with salt and pepper. Place the spaghetti squash in a small bowl and toss with the remaining 1 tablespoon lemon juice. Season to taste with salt and pepper.

ASSEMBLY Layer some of the parsley root, spaghetti squash, and opal basil in the center of each plate. Top with a potato square and repeat until you have 4 layers, ending with a crispy potato square. Place 8 pieces of the pickled beets around the plate and spoon around the golden beet sauce, Basil Oil, and remaining opal basil.

## Wine Notes

Though the mention of pickling may frighten the wine enthusiast, it is not overwhelming in this dish, as the sweetness of the beets seems to balance any acid influence. A clean, unoaky Sauvignon Blanc is best because it allows the basil and parsley root flavors to shine, without interfering with the sweet spaghetti squash. A favorite Napa producer is Groth, a pleasant accompaniment and a great value. Look to the Loire Valley in France: the Côtat Sancerre *Reserve des Monts Damnes* adds a bit more punch and even higher acidity than an American Sauvignon.

# Loquat Ravioli with Vanilla Bean–
# Black Mission Fig Sauce
# and Tart Green Gooseberries

*Pasta for dessert? Why not! Loquats have a delicious, unique flesh, and a flavor that is something like a combination of mango, papaya, and melon. They work beautifully with vanilla, ginger, and lemongrass. Here they are paired with a luscious, heady fig sauce and tart green gooseberries whose sourness works perfectly with the sweet fig and loquat flavors. The chewy pasta rounds out the dish perfectly.*

## Serves 4

*10 black mission figs, cut into quarters*

*1/2 cup plus 1 tablespoon water*

*10 tablespoons sugar*

*2 vanilla beans, split lengthwise with pulp scraped out and reserved*

*16 loquats, peeled and seeded*

*1 cup Sauterne*

*1 egg yolk*

*Vanilla Pasta (recipe follows)*

*1 pint tart green gooseberries*

*3 tablespoons balsamic vinegar*

METHOD Place the figs in a medium saucepan with 1/2 cup of the water and 2 tablespoons of the sugar. Cook over medium heat for 15 to 20 minutes. Purée in a blender until smooth, then pass through a fine-mesh sieve. Return to the saucepan, add the vanilla bean pulp, and continue to cook for 3 minutes on low heat. Finely chop 12 of the loquats. Place 1/2 cup Sauterne and 3 tablespoons of the sugar in a small saucepan and bring to a simmer. Add the diced loquats and continue to cook on low heat for 5 to 7 minutes. Remove the loquats from the pan and cool in a sieve, allowing any excess liquid to drain from the loquats. Reserve the cooking liquid for later use. In a small bowl, whisk together the yolk with the 1 tablespoon of water. Lay the Vanilla

Pasta flat and brush one side with the egg yolk mixture. Place a heaping teaspoon of the cooked loquats on the pasta 2 inches apart, until you have 16 portions. Lay the remaining pasta over the first sheet and filling, and cut out the ravioli. Firmly press the edges together and place on a lightly floured sheet pan. Place in the refrigerator until needed. Thinly slice the remaining loquats. Place the sliced loquats in a small saucepan with the cooking liquid reserved from the diced loquats and warm over medium heat. Place the remaining 1/2 cup Sauterne and 3 tablespoons of the sugar in a small sauté pan. Bring to a simmer and add the gooseberries. Continue to cook for 1 to 2 minutes over medium heat, or until warm. Place the balsamic vinegar in a small saucepan with the remaining 2 tablespoons sugar and cook over low heat for 2 to 3 minutes, or until the sugar is dissolved. Cook the ravioli in boiling salted water until al dente and toss with the cooking liquid from the loquats. Use immediately.

ASSEMBLY Place 4 ravioli in the center of each plate and top them with a mound of gooseberries. Spoon some of the vanilla bean–black mission fig sauce around the plate, along with some of the loquat slices. Spoon the sweetened balsamic over the gooseberries, allowing it to run into the other sauces.

## Vanilla Pasta

Yield: 3/4 pound

*3 eggs*

*2 vanilla beans, split lengthwise with pulp scraped out and reserved*

*2 cups extra-fine semolina flour*

METHOD Gently whisk together the eggs and the vanilla bean pulp in a small bowl. Place the semolina flour in the bowl of an electric mixer and add the egg mixture. Mix on medium until it forms a ball. Wrap the ball in plastic wrap and refrigerate for 1 hour before using. When ready to use, roll the dough out as thin as possible using a pasta machine or rolling by hand. Keep tightly covered until ready to use.

## Wine Notes

Gooseberries are so tart that they upstage any wine's acidity for this delicious combination of flavors. They balance the fig's intense sweetness, a flavor best enhanced by a sweet wine. More modern styles of Tokaji Aszu, like the Château Pajzos 5 Puttonyos, add a rich honeylike quality to the dish. Even sweeter, embellishing the vanilla and fig flavors, would be a sweet late-harvest Riesling. A favorite is the *Pinnacle* by Washington's Blackwood Canyon.

The constant warmth of **July** convinces me to eat ultralight, which requires a welcome shift in focus. I love clean, decisive flavors when it's hot; crunchy and crispy textures win my affection as well. ◊ Perhaps Mother Nature indulges me most this month, providing an array of foods befitting my tendencies. Peppery greens and luscious stone fruits could not be more refreshing in delicate salads. And cucumbers and watermelon are the epitome of invigorating. The textures of daikon and jicama are satisfying yet still light. The first ears of sweet corn, just plucked from the stalks, and chanterelle mushrooms, gathered from the forest floor, are laden with their own distinctive flavors. Boniato, the tropical white sweet potato, and tiny teardrop tomatoes are glorious at this time of the year. And my favorite fruit of all—white peaches—are plump, and perfectly decadent. The clean flavors of high summer make for light eating with no regrets.

# Fennel-Apple Salad with Fennel Purée, Fennel Sauce, Apple Chips, and Mustard Seed Vinaigrette

*Apple, mustard, and fennel are a fantastic combination of flavors—sweet, spicy and anise melding together perfectly. The apple is introduced twice, both in raw and in oven-dried pieces. The fennel actually comes into play three times, first with the sauce, then with the little julienned salad, and finally, with the delicate, satiny purée. If a more substantial dish is desired, beef tenderloin or chicken breast could be added with superb results.*

## Serves 4

*1¹⁄₂ cups chopped Spanish onions*

*2 tablespoons butter*

*1 cup peeled and chopped Granny Smith apple*

*4 cups chopped fennel bulbs*

*3 cups water*

*Salt and pepper*

*2 cups fennel fronds, blanched and shocked*

*1 cup finely julienned fennel*

*1 cup finely julienned Granny Smith apple, with skin*

*Mustard Seed Vinaigrette (recipe follows)*

*1 tablespoon chopped fennel fronds*

*12 Apple Chips (see Appendices)*

METHOD Sweat 1 cup of the onion with 1 tablespoon of the butter in a medium sauté pan until translucent. Add the chopped apple and 3 cups of the chopped fennel. Continue to sauté for 5 to 7 minutes, or until the fennel begins to soften. Add 2 cups of the water and continue to cook for 20 to 25 minutes, or until most of the liquid has been absorbed and the fennel is extremely tender. Remove the mixture from the pan and purée in a blender until smooth. (If the mixture appears too wet, dry it out on the stove in a nonstick pan until it has a slightly stiff consistency.) Season to taste with salt and pepper.

Place the remaining ¹⁄₂ cup chopped onion in a small sauté pan with the remaining 1 tablespoon butter and sweat until translucent. Add the remaining 1 cup chopped fennel and cook for 5 to 7 minutes. Add ³⁄₄ cup water and continue to cook until tender. Remove from the pan and cool. Place the blanched fennel fronds in the blender with the cooled fennel-onion mixture and the remaining ¹⁄₄ cup of water. Blend until smooth and season to taste with salt and pepper.

Toss the julienned fennel, apple, and half of the Mustard Seed Vinaigrette in a medium bowl and season to taste with salt and pepper.

ASSEMBLY Place some of the green fennel purée in a pool in the center of each plate and place 3 quenelles of the fennel-apple purée at three points. In the center, place a mound of the julienned fennel-apple salad. Place an Apple Chip standing upright in the center of each quenelle, leaning toward the center and each other. Spoon some of the remaining Mustard Seed Vinaigrette around the plate and top with freshly ground black pepper.

## Mustard Seed Vinaigrette

Yield: 8 tablespoons

*2 teaspoons Dijon-style mustard*

*1 tablespoon rice vinegar*

*¹⁄₄ cup olive oil*

*2 teaspoons water*

*1 tablespoon mustard seed*

*Salt and pepper*

METHOD Place the mustard and vinegar in a small bowl. Slowly whisk in the olive oil and thin with the water. Stir in the mustard seed and season to taste with salt and pepper.

## Wine Notes

This salad requires a crisp wine with evident fruit but light oak influences. Sauvignon Blanc–based wines from Morgan and Carmenet in California are pleasant, as they exhibit a touch of oak and match the apple emphasis of the salad. Ideal, however, is a small production wine from Chappellet, its *Old Vine Cuvée* made from Chenin Blanc. The wine is assertively fruity and its slight oak component adds complexity to the finishing flavors of the salad.

# Roasted Red and Yellow Teardrop Tomatoes with Caviar, Yukon Gold Potato Purée, and Roasted Shallot Vinaigrette

*The creamy Yukon gold potato purée is the perfect foil for the decadent caviar and the playfully acidic teardrop tomatoes which balance the elegant sweet, roasted shallot vinaigrette. Altogether, the result is one of terrific complexity, yet harmony, of flavor and texture.*

**Serves 4**

*3 shallots, peeled*

*½ cup olive oil*

*1 Yukon gold potato (about 8 ounces), peeled and cut into 1-inch dice*

*4 tablespoons butter*

*2 to 3 tablespoons heavy cream*

*Salt and pepper*

*2 teaspoons rice vinegar*

*2 tablespoons chopped flat-leaf parsley*

*1 pint red teardrop tomatoes, peeled*

*1 pint yellow teardrop tomatoes, peeled*

*2 tablespoons Osetra caviar (optional)*

*1 tablespoon chives, cut in 1-inch-long pieces*

METHOD Place the shallots and olive oil in an ovenproof pan and roast at 375 degrees for 1 to 1½ hours, or until the shallots are extremely soft. Place the potatoes in a medium saucepan, cover with cold salted water, and simmer for 15 to 20 minutes, or until the potatoes are tender. Drain, and place in a medium mixing bowl with the butter and cream. Stir until smooth (if there are any lumps, pass it through a fine-mesh sieve) and season to taste with salt and pepper.

Place the vinegar in a small mixing bowl and slowly whisk in 5 tablespoons of the olive oil that was cooked with the shallots. Season to taste with salt and pepper. Remove and discard the outer layer of the shallots, slice thinly, and add to the vinaigrette along with the parsley. Place the tomatoes in an ovenproof pan with the remaining olive oil from the shallots. Roast in the oven at 375 degrees for 10 to 15 minutes, or until hot. Remove from the pan and toss the tomatoes with the caviar in a small mixing bowl.

ASSEMBLY Place some of the Yukon gold potato purée in the center of each plate. Spoon some of the caviar tomatoes over the potatoes. Spoon the roasted-shallot vinaigrette around the plate and top with the chives.

## Wine Notes

Rich, ripe California Chardonnay seems the most useful match to the Yukon gold potatoes, especially with the decadent touch of caviar. The tomatoes become an accent of textural and acid counterpoint, and seem not to interfere with the full-throttle, fat Chardonnay of Talbott or Marcassin. Oak also marries well with the shallots' sweetness. Certain older Hermitage Blanc could also be appropriate, as they mature more into a Burgundy style and lose their young aromatic personality.

# Baby White Carrots, Roasted Lipstick Peppers, and White Trumpet Mushroom Ragout with Beef Stock Reduction

*When I eat a dish like this I certainly do not need meat or fish.*
*This preparation is earthy and full of lusty richness and it does not in any way leave one*
*yearning for more. The combination of the carrots, the tiny sweet peppers,*
*the delicate but meaty mushrooms, and the meat stock reduction combine perfectly.*
*Each flavor seems to naturally bind to the others as though they were meant to be together.*
*A final poignant touch comes by adding a few daikon sprouts and a twist of black pepper.*

**Serves** 4

*2 tablespoons butter*

*2 teaspoons chopped shallots*

*1 cup roasted white trumpet mushrooms*
*(see Appendices)*

*2 teaspoons freshly squeezed lemon juice*

*Salt and pepper*

*12 baby white carrots, blanched*

*1 cup sorrel, cut into fine chiffonade*

*1 tablespoon olive oil*

*8 lipstick peppers, roasted and cleaned*

*1/4 cup Beef Stock Reduction*
*(see Appendices)*

*1/4 cup daikon sprouts*

*4 teaspoons Basil Oil (see Appendices)*

METHOD Place 1 tablespoon of the butter and the shallots in a medium sauté pan and sweat until translucent. Add the mushrooms and 2 teaspoons lemon juice and sauté over medium-high heat until lightly caramelized. Season to taste with salt and pepper.

Place the remaining 1 tablespoon butter and the white carrots in another sauté pan. Cook over medium heat until lightly golden and season to taste with salt and pepper.

Toss the sorrel with the olive oil in a small bowl and season to taste with salt and pepper. Cut the tops off the red peppers and gently remove the seeds. Stuff the peppers with the sorrel and bake at 350 degrees for 5 minutes, or until hot. Warm the Beef Stock Reduction in a small saucepan.

ASSEMBLY Place one of the sorrel-stuffed peppers in the center of each plate and layer with some of the mushrooms, carrots, and daikon sprouts. Place a second pepper on top of the ragout and top with the remaining carrots, mushrooms, and daikon sprouts. Spoon some of the Beef Stock Reduction and Basil Oil around the plate.

## Wine Notes

The flavor of peppers and sorrel is assertive here and independently well matched by clean, assertive Sauvignon Blanc. But the sweetness of the delicate white carrots and the slight richness of the mushrooms can support a low tannin red wine, especially with the Beef Stock Reduction. Cool Chinon, a fresh and vibrant Cabernet-Franc—based red from France's Loire Valley, matches the freshness of flavor here while being "red" enough for the meat juices. The best example is a young Chinon from Joguet.

# Pepper Cress and Rainbow Radishes Salad
## with White Peaches, Mariposa Plums,
## and Balsamic Red Onions

*This salad is very refreshing and is quite easy to prepare.*
*Everything is simply cut up and tossed together. The pepper cress has a pleasant, assertive bite,*
*the radishes are cleansing and crispy, the plums are sweet and sensual, the oven-dried*
*white peach pieces add a concentrated mature richness, and the shallots add an elegant earthiness.*
*In summer I love salads composed of fruit and spicy lettuces; they satisfy like nothing else.*

**Serves 4**

*4 white peaches, peeled*
*1 small red onion, thinly sliced*
*2 tablespoons balsamic vinegar*
*3 tablespoons olive oil*
*Salt and pepper*
*¼ cup water*
*2 teaspoons rice vinegar*
*3 Mariposa plums, peeled*
*2 white radishes, thinly sliced*
*2 pink radishes, thinly sliced*
*2 purple radishes, thinly sliced*
*3 cups pepper cress*
*1½ teaspoons freshly squeezed lemon juice*

METHOD  Slice 1 of the peaches into ½-inch wedges. Place on a nonstick sheet pan and bake at 200 degrees for 40 minutes. Flip the peach pieces over and continue to dry out for 30 to 40 minutes, or until lightly golden brown. Toss the red onion, balsamic vinegar, and 2 teaspoons of the olive oil in a small bowl. Season with salt and pepper.

Place in an ovenproof pan and bake at 375 degrees for 20 to 25 minutes, or until all of the balsamic has been absorbed by the red onion. Remove from oven and allow to cool completely. To make the vinaigrette, coarsely chop one of the peaches and place in a blender with the water; purée until smooth, then strain through a fine-mesh sieve and place in a small bowl. Slowly whisk in the remaining 2 tablespoons and 1 teaspoon of olive oil and the rice vinegar and season to taste with salt and pepper. Cut 1 of the plums into small dice, and thinly slice the remaining 2 plums. Cut ½ of one of the peaches into a small dice and thinly slice the remaining 1½ peaches. Place the sliced radishes, plums, and peaches, along with the pepper cress and balsamic red onions in a medium bowl. Gently toss together with 3 tablespoons of the vinaigrette and the lemon juice. Season to taste with salt and pepper.

ASSEMBLY  Place a mound of the salad in the center of each plate and arrange the diced fruit around the salad. Spoon a ring of the peach vinaigrette around the plate and top with freshly ground black pepper.

**Wine Notes**

Vegetable flavors (caramelized onion, radish, pepper cress) balance the oozy peach and plum ripeness in this salad, and the wine choice needs to embellish these flavors. The spicy, floral sweetness of a light Gewürztraminer from California makes the best match. The Babcock Santa Ynez Gewürztraminer emphasizes the sweet peach and plum flavors and its slight minor chord of bitterness does well with the spicy radish and pepper cress. Alsatian styles of Gewürztraminer are generally too intense. For something completely different, try an Austrian Sauvignon Blanc from Styria. The Tement *Zieregg* is ripe and juicy yet un-oaked and without the attendant grassy or herbal notes that plague lesser Sauvignons. This is a wine of great clarity and purity.

# Chilled Clear Cucumber Soup with Watermelon, Apple, and Jicama

*A preparation like this is the epitome of a summertime dish—light, refreshing, healthful,
and simple to prepare, with lots of texture and flavor. Aside from the cool, pure, intense cucumber-
flavored broth, what I really love about this dish is the texture of all of the vegetables.
For a more substantial luncheon preparation you could easily add a
piece of cold poached salmon or some lobster meat.*

**Serves 4**

*2 English cucumbers*

*Salt and pepper*

*2 tablespoons yogurt*

*1 teaspoon freshly squeezed lemon juice*

*1/2 teaspoon togarashi*

*1/4 cup peeled, 1-inch-long julienned cucumber*

*1/4 cup peeled, 1-inch-long julienned green apple*

*8 teaspoons diced watermelon, seeds removed*

*8 teaspoons diced yellow watermelon, seeds removed*

*1/4 cup diced avocado*

*8 teaspoons diced jicama*

*8 teaspoons diced tomatillo*

*8 teaspoons Oven-Dried Tomato (see Appendices)*

*4 teaspoons fresh dill*

*4 teaspoons Dill Oil*

METHOD Cut one of the English cucumbers into eight 1-inch pieces. Using a round cutter or a paring knife, remove the skin from the cucumber. Hollow out the inside of the cucumber pieces using a Parisian scoop to make 8 cups. Transfer the pulp to a blender with the remaining cucumber and 1 teaspoon salt, and purée until smooth. Strain the cucumber purée through 3 layers of cheesecloth, letting it sit in the refrigerator until all of the liquid has passed through. Season with salt if necessary and keep refrigerated until needed. Place the cucumber cups in a small saucepan with 1 cup of water and bring to a simmer for 1 minute. Remove from the pan and cool completely. Combine the yogurt, lemon juice, and togarashi in a small bowl. Place the julienned cucumber and apple in a separate small bowl and toss with the yogurt mixture.

ASSEMBLY Place 2 of the cucumber cups in the center of each bowl. Fill each cup with some of the julienned cucumber and apple mixture. Place the diced watermelon, avocado, jicama, and tomatillo around the cucumber cups. Ladle some of the cold cucumber broth in each bowl and sprinkle the fresh dill on top of the broth. Drizzle 1 teaspoon Dill Oil in each bowl and top with freshly ground pepper.

**Wine Notes**

The melon influence here adds sweetness and balance to the savory elements of cucumber and tomatillo. The wine choice should parallel this effect. Some dry Alsatian Rieslings like Ostertag's *Muenchberg* or the *Herrenweg* by Zind Humbrecht come close to this parallel, but more sweetness is needed, along with high acidity, to maintain the fresh, light feel of the soup. Mosel Rieslings offer these characteristics. Even more precisely, Saar and Ruwer Rieslings are impressive. The great von Schubert Ruwer estate, responsible for the exciting Maximin Gruenhaus Rieslings, makes the perfect foil, its Abtsberg Kabinett, whose raciness and slight apple-like sweetness elevate the humble components of this soup to a sensational pleasure.

# Macaroni Timbales in the Style of Fredy Girardet with Boniato, Sweet Corn, and Chanterelle Mushrooms

*This dish is inspired by a preparation I had in July 1995 at the Restaurant Girardet,
one of my very favorite restaurants in the world. Chef Girardet's version of the macaroni
timbale included rabbit, sweetbreads, and wild mushrooms.
I have omitted the meat and added sweet corn and boniato, the white sweet potato
found in the Caribbean and in parts of Central America.
The sweet corn and the boniato provide a wonderful sweetness, the chanterelles
a profound earthiness, and the neutral pasta grounds everything with its heartiness.
Finally a touch of saffron lends the perfect restrained poetry.*

**Serves 4**

*1 (8-ounce) boniato (white sweet potato)*

*6 tablespoons butter*

*Salt and pepper*

*6 ears sweet corn, kernels removed
and cobs reserved*

*½ teaspoon saffron*

*1 tablespoon chopped flat-leaf parsley*

*1 tablespoon chopped opal basil*

*4 teaspoons marjoram leaves*

*2 tablespoons chopped Spanish onion*

*¼ cup water*

*2 cups roasted chanterelle mushrooms*

*2 teaspoons chopped shallots*

*6 ounces ziti, cooked and tossed with
2 tablespoons olive oil*

METHOD  Place the boniato in a medium saucepan and cover with cold salted water. Simmer for 12 to 15 minutes, or until tender. Drain and place in a medium bowl with 3 tablespoons of the butter. Using a fork, coarsely mash the boniato and season to taste with salt and pepper. Place the corn cobs and half of the kernels in a medium saucepan and cover with water. Simmer for 1 hour. Strain through a fine-mesh sieve and discard the cobs and corn. Place the corn stock in a small saucepan with two-thirds of the saffron. Bring to a simmer and reduce for 10 to 12 minutes, or until you have about 1½ cups of corn broth. Add the parsley, basil, half of the marjoram, and season to taste with salt and pepper.

In a small saucepan, sweat the onion with 2 tablespoons of the butter until translucent. Add the remaining corn and the water. Continue to cook with the remaining saffron for 10 to 15 minutes, or until tender, and season to taste with salt and pepper.

Sauté the mushrooms and shallots with the remaining 1 tablespoon butter and season to taste with salt and pepper. Place four 2-inch-high ring molds on a sheet pan and place the tubes of pasta standing upright side-by-side around the inside of the mold to form the timbales. Place about ¼ cup of the boniato in the bottom of the mold and press down to secure the pasta. Spoon in some of the corn and top with the sautéed mushrooms. Bake in the oven at 375 degrees for 5 to 10 minutes, until hot.

ASSEMBLY  Place the pasta timbale in the center of each plate and carefully remove the mold. Spoon the remaining corn and herb-infused corn broth around the plate. Sprinkle the remaining marjoram on top of the mushrooms. Top with freshly ground black pepper.

## Wine Notes

Rich and oaky Sauvignon Blanc is useful here. Sweet corn and the sweet boniato make the wood flavors harmonize and the variety is less cloying than Chardonnay would be with the dish. Graves Blanc with a few years' aging can be satisfying— Château Couhins Lurton 1989 is good. (The usually pleasing Blanc de Lynch Bages yields a slight honeyed flavor that does not resolve well with this dish.) An American wine that could work well is the Langtry Meritage White, a generously oaked, flashy Sauvignon Blanc–based wine in the Graves tradition.

# Warm Berry Compote with Fraises des Bois and Lemon Verbena Ice Cream "Cannelloni"

*Few things are better than perfectly ripe berries gently warmed and served with their own juices.*
*In this recipe I have done just that but have also added a wonderfully fragrant lemon verbena*
*ice cream and a peppery cannelloni-shaped tuile. The satiny ice cream with its haunting perfume*
*and the peppery tuile add complex, and complementary, elements to the warm berries.*
*A little drizzle of verbena syrup gives the berry juices just the right amount of added sweetness.*

### Serves 4

*½ cup huckleberries*
*½ cup blackberries*
*½ cup raspberries*
*½ cup water*
*½ cup red currants*
*½ cup Black Corinth grapes*
*½ cup white fraises des bois*
*½ cup red fraises des bois*
*4 Black Pepper Tuiles (recipe follows)*
*Lemon Verbena Ice Cream (recipe follows)*
*Lemon Verbena Syrup (recipe follows)*

METHOD  Place the huckleberries, blackberries, raspberries, and water in a medium sauté pan and gently cook over medium heat for 2 minutes. Add the currants and grapes and continue to cook for 1 minute. With a spoon, gently remove the berries from the pan and toss with the fraises des bois. Over medium heat, reduce the berry juices by half.

ASSEMBLY  Place some of the berries and the berry sauce in the center of each plate. Using a small scoop or spoon, carefully fill each of the tuiles with the ice cream and place on top of the berries. Drizzle Lemon Verbena Syrup around the tuiles.

### Black Pepper Tuiles

Yield: 4 to 6

*¼ cup sugar*
*5 tablespoons flour*
*3 egg whites*
*5 tablespoons melted butter, at room temperature*
*Pinch of salt*
*1 teaspoon freshly ground black pepper*

METHOD  Combine the sugar and flour in a mixing bowl, then stir in the egg whites, melted butter, salt, and pepper. Chill for 30 minutes. Lightly oil the back side of a 12 by 16-inch sheet pan. Spread a thin, even layer of the tuile batter on the back side of the sheet pan, covering the whole area. Bake at 300 degrees for 8 to 12 minutes, or until the batter turns just golden brown. Quickly remove from the oven and, using a pizza cutter, square off the baked batter. Then cut into 4 or 6 rectangles 4 by 5 inches. (You may have a few extra, but this is good since they are extremely fragile.) Return to the oven for 30 seconds to soften the tuiles so they will easily mold. Remove the rectangles one at a time and, using your hand, gently form 4-inch-long cylinders. Store in an airtight container at room temperature until ready to use.

### Lemon Verbena Ice Cream

Yield: 3 cups

*1½ cups heavy cream*
*¾ cup milk*
*¾ cup half-and-half*
*3 cups lemon verbena*
*6 egg yolks*
*¾ cup plus 2 tablespoons sugar*

METHOD  Combine the heavy cream, milk, and half-and-half in a medium saucepan. Bring to a boil over medium heat. Add the lemon verbena and let sit for 10 minutes. Remove the lemon verbena and set aside. Whisk the yolks and the sugar together in a medium bowl, temper the mixture with the hot cream, and return to the saucepan. Cook over medium heat for 2 minutes while stirring constantly. Strain through a fine-mesh sieve. Place in the blender with the lemon verbena and purée until smooth. Strain again through a fine-mesh sieve. Cool completely and freeze in an ice cream machine. Keep frozen until ready to use.

### Lemon Verbena Syrup

Yield: ½ cup

*½ cup sugar*
*½ cup water*
*1 cup lemon verbena, blanched and shocked*

METHOD  Place the sugar and water in a small saucepan, bring to a simmer, then remove from heat and cool completely. Place the lemon verbena in the blender with the cooled simple syrup. Purée until bright green, about 2 minutes. Pour into a container and refrigerate overnight. Strain through a fine-mesh sieve and keep refrigerated until needed.

### Wine Notes

This dessert uses unusual savory elements to balance the sweetness of the berries and rich ice cream. The wine choice should reflect these, and be quite sweet as well. Château St. Jean, a well-established leader in dessert wines from California, has produced numerous late harvest Gewürztraminers, and their Select Late Harvest Gewürztraminer *Frank Johnson Vineyard* 1992 makes an amazing flavor statement alongside the odd lemon verbena and pepper pungency. The sweetness level (14.7 percent residual sugar) is ideal, and the varietal characteristics of Gewürztraminer are well preserved.

In the dog days of summer, I am drawn to foods with slightly elevated acid—such as pickled vegetables, caper berries, and spicy giardiniera—because they add zing to various dishes. At the same time, I crave salads composed of fruits with differing textures and flavor characteristics. Fortunately, **August** delivers in both regards.

Consider just a few of the month's most magnificent foods: Heirloom tomatoes reach their zenith and merely need to be sliced and sprinkled with salt to become a truly profound gustatory experience. Corn peaks in richness and sweetness, and can be blended into soups to be served warm or chilled. The unusual lobster mushroom adds a sophisticated complexity to soups, grain-based preparations, and ragouts. Bing cherries are at their fullest and juiciest, as are golden raspberries. And cilantro and lemon basil are versatile, full-flavored herbs excellent for late-summer cooking. These heat-soaked days are perfect for truly savoring the summer's penultimate offerings.

# Asian Pear–Heirloom Tomato Salad and Red Fortune Plums with Spicy Apricot–Chestnut Honey Sauce

*Fruit salads are wonderfully refreshing, and with just a little pepper or spice, the flavors of the fruits are accentuated. For those hot August days, this salad works perfectly as a light appetizer. Pairing the sweet, luscious tomatoes with the playfully tart plums and the sweet-and-sour apricot dressing really brings out the magic of each element, and the black sesame seeds add an important textural contrast.*

**Serves 4**

*3 apricots, peeled and chopped*

*½ jalapeño, seeded*

*½ cup water*

*½ cup apricot juice*

*1 tablespoon chestnut honey*

*1 heirloom tomato (such as Purple Cherokee or Brandy Wine), cut into batons*

*2 teaspoons olive oil*

*Salt and pepper*

*2 Friar plums, cut into wedges*

*2 Red Fortune plums, cut into wedges*

*1 Asian pear, cut into batons*

*1 teaspoon black sesame seeds*

*3 tablespoons freshly squeezed orange juice*

*1 teaspoon togarashi*

*¼ teaspoon sea salt*

*¾ cup golden raspberries*

*2 tablespoons fresh lemon basil, cut into fine chiffonade*

*2 heaping tablespoons macadamia nuts, roasted and thinly sliced*

METHOD Place the chopped apricots, jalapeño, and water in a small saucepan and simmer for 30 minutes. Place in a blender, purée until smooth, and strain through a fine-mesh sieve. In a small saucepan, simmer the apricot juice and honey over medium heat for 15 minutes, or until reduced by half. Add to the purée and stir until incorporated. In a small bowl, toss the tomato batons with the olive oil and season to taste with salt and pepper. In another bowl, mix the plums, Asian pear, black sesame seeds, orange juice, togarashi, and sea salt just to combine.

ASSEMBLY Place some of the plum mixture, tomato pieces, and golden raspberries in the center of each plate. Top with the lemon basil and macadamia nuts. Spoon some of the juices from the bowl on top of the fruit and spoon the apricot-honey purée around the plate.

## Wine Notes

These delicious tomatoes are as much a sweet fruity presence as the plums and pears. The accompanying wine should interlock these fruits without dominating them. A number of Chenin Blanc–based wines are useful: Husch Anderson Valley, Foreau Vouvray Sec, even a slightly sweet Bonnezeaux from Château de Fesles in the Loire Valley are tasty pear/peach-aroma wines. The richness of Caymus *Conundrum* (88 percent barrel fermented) makes a rather different statement with this salad, though the heady Viognier portion of this wine can be as much of a turn-off as a turn-on.

# Pea Sprouts, Shiitake Mushrooms, Pickled Cucumber, and Tofu Stir-Fry with Jasmine Rice, Miso Sauce, and Coriander Juice

*Stir-fries are easy and quick and can be altered to fit any taste.*
*This preparation has many wonderful textures and flavors all melding together perfectly.*
*Small strips of chicken could easily be added to create a heartier effect.*
*The greatest part of this dish, though, may very well be the jasmine rice, with its subtle perfume.*

**Serves 4**

*2 small pickling cucumbers*

*1 cup plus 3 tablespoons Pickling Juice (see Appendices)*

*1/2 cup tofu, cut into 1/2-inch cubes*

*1/2 cup liquid from tofu package*

*2 tablespoons plus 1/4 teaspoon tamari soy sauce*

*1 tablespoon white miso paste*

*1 cup (about 4 ounces) shiitake mushrooms, stemmed and julienned*

*3 tablespoons sesame oil*

*2 tablespoons pickled ginger, chopped*

*1 cup (about 4 ounces) mung bean sprouts*

*1 1/2 cups (about 4 ounces) pea sprouts*

*1/2 cup (about 1 ounce) wheat grass, cut into 1-inch-long pieces*

*2 tablespoons chopped fresh coriander*

*Salt and pepper*

*2 cups hot cooked jasmine rice*

*Coriander Juice (recipe follows)*

*Coriander Oil (see Appendices)*

METHOD Slice the cucumbers lengthwise then into 1/4-inch crescents. Place in a medium bowl and add 1 cup Pickling Juice.

Place in the refrigerator for at least 2 hours.

In a small bowl, combine the tofu, the liquid from the tofu, and 2 tablespoons of the tamari. Marinate for 1 hour in the refrigerator.

Place the miso in a small bowl and whisk in the remaining 3 tablespoons of Pickling Juice and the tamari. Sauté the shiitake mushrooms in the sesame oil over high heat until golden brown. Add the marinated tofu, pickled cucumbers, and pickled ginger and continue cooking for 2 to 3 minutes. Add the mung bean sprouts, pea sprouts, wheat grass, and chopped coriander and continue to cook but only until they begin to wilt. Season to taste with salt and pepper.

ASSEMBLY Place some of the hot jasmine rice in the center of each plate inside a 3-inch ring mold. Place some of the stir-fried vegetables on top of the rice and remove the mold. Spoon some of the miso sauce, Coriander Juice, and Coriander Oil around the plate. Top with freshly ground black pepper.

**Coriander Juice**

Yield: about 1/2 cup

*2 cups packed fresh coriander, blanched*

*3 tablespoons water*

*2 tablespoons grapeseed oil*

*2 tablespoons olive oil*

*Salt and pepper*

METHOD Squeeze any excess water from the coriander and place in a blender with the water and oil. Purée for 3 to 4 minutes, or until smooth. Strain through a fine-mesh sieve and season to taste with salt and pepper. Refrigerate until ready to use.

**Wine Notes**

Jasmine rice is somewhat sweet and the sesame flavor can stand some oak. The best wine should play to these flavors. Several vintages of Chassagne-Montrachets from Michel Colin-Deleger have impressed us over time with their unmistakable oak signature yet plenty of respect for *terroir*. The pickling flavor here is mild and the effect of the coriander is not so jarring as to require a leaner wine; better balance is achieved, however, with a 1993 or 1991 than with the opulent 1992s.

# Sweet Corn Soup
## with Grilled Lobster Mushrooms and Shellfish Oil

~~~~~~~~~~~~~~~~~~~~~~~~~~~~~~~~~~~~~~~~~~~~~~~~~~~~~~~~

*Sweet corn and lobster is one of the all-time great flavor combinations. Here, though,*
*I create the taste of lobster meat with the complexly flavored lobster mushrooms. The actual lobster,*
*or shellfish, flavor is introduced by a little drizzle of Shellfish Oil. Green onions not only*
*add wonderful texture, but their flavor cuts nicely into the woody grilled flavors of the mushrooms.*

**Serves 4**

*8 ounces lobster mushrooms*

*¼ cup olive oil*

*3 garlic cloves, sliced*

*Salt and pepper*

*12 ears of corn, kernels removed and cobs reserved*

*2 tablespoons butter*

*1 Spanish onion, finely diced*

*4 green onions, blanched and cut into ½-inch pieces on the bias*

*4 teaspoons Shellfish Oil (recipe follows)*

*4 teaspoons chives, cut into ½-inch-long pieces*

METHOD  Rinse the lobster mushrooms and toss with the olive oil and garlic. Season with salt and pepper and let sit in the refrigerator for 1 hour. Grill the mushrooms over moderate heat for 7 to 10 minutes, or until tender. Remove from the grill and slice into ¼-inch-thick pieces.

Place all of the corn cobs and half the corn kernels in a large saucepan, cover with water, and simmer for 1 hour. Strain through a fine-mesh sieve, discarding the cobs and kernels. Transfer the corn broth to a smaller saucepan and simmer for about 40 minutes, or until reduced to 3 cups. Place 5 teaspoons of the butter and the diced onion in a large sauté pan and sweat over medium heat until translucent. Add the remaining corn kernels and continue to cook for 12 to 15 minutes, or until tender. Season to taste with salt and pepper. Reserve 1 cup of the cooked corn and place the remaining corn in a blender with the corn broth; purée until smooth. Strain through a fine-mesh sieve and season to taste with salt and pepper. Warm the green onions in 1 teaspoon of the butter over medium heat, and season to taste with salt and pepper. Reheat the corn soup before serving.

ASSEMBLY  Ladle some of the soup in each bowl and place some of the green onions in the center. Lay the sliced mushrooms on top of the onions and spoon the remaining corn kernels on top of the mushrooms. Drizzle the Shellfish Oil around the mushrooms and sprinkle the chives in the bowl. Top with freshly ground black pepper.

## Shellfish Oil

Yield: about 2 cups

*½ cup chopped carrots*

*½ cup chopped celery*

*½ cup chopped onion*

*2 cups grapeseed oil*

*2 tablespoons tomato paste*

*1 pound fresh lobster or crayfish shells, chopped*

METHOD  Caramelize the vegetables and 2 tablespoons of the grapeseed oil in a large sauté pan. Add the tomato paste and continue to cook for 3 to 4 minutes. Add the fresh shells and the remaining oil and simmer for 25 minutes. Cool and store overnight in the refrigerator. Strain through a fine-mesh sieve and store in the refrigerator until ready to use.

### Wine Notes

An absolutely stunning combination of flavors gives this soup an intensity and richness not often seen in vegetable dishes, and consequently the wine choices should be richer and more opulently oaky than most. A ripe white Burgundy or a full-bodied Chardonnay will accompany the rich mushroom flavor, and oak will match the sweetness of the corn soup. Try a great Chevalier-Montrachet from Niellon or the amazing Matanzas Creek *Journey*—either of these rare wines from the 1992 vintage will be wonderful.

# Arugula Noodles with Smoked Yellow Tomato Sauce, Black Olives, and Roasted Garlic Purée

*I love the peppery flavor and the elegant sharpness of arugula. It is satisfying and refreshing in the heat of August. In this dish there are several lusty yet refined flavors that all meld together superbly. Sweet oven-roasted tomatoes; salty black olives; smoked, barely acidic tomato sauce; creamy roasted garlic purée; and the spicy arugula all play off each other with glorious results.*

**Serves 4**

*Arugula Noodles (recipe follows)*

*3 tablespoons olive oil*

*8 ounces arugula, washed, stemmed, and coarsely chopped*

*Salt and pepper*

*½ cup Oven-Dried Tomatoes (see Appendices)*

*Smoked Yellow Tomato Sauce (recipe follows), heated*

*16 oil-cured French black olives, pitted and cut into quarters*

*¼ cup Roasted Garlic Purée (see Appendices)*

*Arugula Oil (recipe follows)*

METHOD Cook the Arugula Noodles in boiling salted water for 2 to 3 minutes, or until al dente. Toss the noodles with the olive oil and arugula, allowing the arugula to wilt in the hot noodles. Season to taste with salt and pepper. Coarsely chop the Oven-Dried Tomatoes.

ASSEMBLY In the center of each plate, place a large circle of the hot Smoked Yellow Tomato Sauce. Using a long fork, twist the Arugula Noodles into a mound and place in the center of the sauce. Arrange the olives and tomato pieces around the pasta and spoon some of the Roasted Garlic Purée and Arugula Oil around the plate. Top with freshly ground black pepper.

## Arugula Noodles

Yield: ¾ pound

*8 ounces arugula, stemmed, blanched, and shocked*

*2 eggs, lightly beaten*

*2 to 2½ cups semolina flour*

METHOD Squeeze all of the excess water out of the arugula and pat dry with paper towels. Place in a blender with the eggs and purée for about 2 minutes, or until incorporated. Place 2 cups of the semolina flour and the egg mixture in a mixing bowl fitted with the dough hook. On medium speed, mix until it forms a solid mass; if it is too wet, add the remaining flour. Form into a ball, cover with plastic wrap, and place in the refrigerator for 30 minutes. Roll out on a lightly floured surface by hand, or use a pasta machine to a thickness of about ¹⁄₁₆ of an inch. Cut the pasta sheet into fettuccine noodles.

## Arugula Oil

Yield: about ½ cup

*4 ounces arugula, stemmed, blanched, and shocked*

*¼ cup grapeseed oil*

*½ cup olive oil*

METHOD Place the arugula and the two oils in a blender and purée for about 3 minutes, or until bright green. Place in the refrigerator and let sit 24 hours. Strain through a fine-mesh sieve and let sit another 24 hours in the refrigerator. Decant.

## Smoked Yellow Tomato Sauce

*6 ounces hickory wood chips*

*3 medium yellow tomatoes, peeled and cut into quarters*

*1 Spanish onion, diced*

*2 tablespoons butter*

*Salt and pepper*

METHOD Soak half of the wood chips in 1 cup of water for 1 hour. Drain the excess water and set aside. Place the dry chips in the base of a grill or smoker. Using a propane torch, light the dry chips until you get a strong smoke. Add the wet chips. Place the tomatoes on the rack above the chips and cover. You may need to check every 15 minutes to make sure you still have a heavy smoke going. Continue to smoke the tomatoes for 1½ to 2 hours, or until they have a strong smoky flavor.

In a medium saucepan, sweat the onions and butter over medium heat until translucent. Coarsely chop the smoked tomatoes, add them to the saucepan, and continue to cook for 20 to 30 minutes, or until most of the liquid from the tomatoes is reduced. Place the hot tomato mixture in a blender, purée until smooth, and season to taste with salt and pepper.

## Wine Notes

Here Mediterranean ingredients (or Californian, for that matter) combine for an effect of sweet smokiness with some bitterness from the olives. While Fino Sherry like Tio Pepe is useful for these flavors, more appropriate for the dish's probable position in the meal would be a dry Rosé. Grenache-based Rosés from the South of France are a bit peppery and emphasize the bitter elements of arugula and olive. A more seamless match is the Castello di Ama Rosato, made from Sangiovese, or the Cotat Sancerre-Chavignol Rosé, made from Pinot Noir. These wines are absolutely dry; off-dry pink wines, such as White Zinfandel or Portuguese Rosés, will be cloying.

# Goat Cheese–Stuffed Miniature Red and Green Tomatoes with Red Bell Pepper Juice and Caper Berries

*If plain goat cheese is fabulous, then warm goat cheese is truly heavenly.*
*I especially like it when combined with such classic elements as tomatoes and basil.*
*In this preparation I have added roasted pine nuts for a touch of richness,*
*caper berries for piquancy, and red bell pepper juice for a complex sweetness.*

**Serves 4**

*8 ounces goat cheese (such as Capriole)*

*4 tablespoons opal basil, cut into fine chiffonade*

*Salt and pepper*

*12 miniature red tomatoes, peeled, tops removed, and centers hollowed out*

*8 miniature green tomatoes, peeled, tops removed, and centers hollowed out*

*3 to 4 tablespoons water*

*4 teaspoons olive oil*

*¼ cup caper berries, thinly sliced*

*4 teaspoons pine nuts, roasted until golden brown*

*4 teaspoons Red Bell Pepper Juice (see Appendices)*

*4 teaspoons Basil Oil (see Appendices)*

METHOD  Place 6 ounces of the goat cheese in a small bowl, fold in 2 teaspoons of the opal basil, and season to taste with salt and pepper.

Place the tomatoes on a sheet pan and season with salt and pepper. Fill the tomatoes with the goat cheese mixture. Bake at 375 degrees for 10 to 12 minutes. To make the goat cheese cream, place the remaining goat cheese in a small bowl, whisk in the water, and season to taste with salt and pepper.

ASSEMBLY  In the center of each plate, place 3 red and 2 green tomatoes. Drizzle the olive oil over the tomatoes. Place the caper berries, pine nuts, and remaining opal basil around the tomatoes. Spoon some of the goat cheese cream, Red Bell Pepper Juice, and Basil Oil around the plate. Top with freshly ground black pepper.

## Wine Notes

The intense tartness and high acidity of the capers present a difficult challenge, but the creaminess of the goat cheese allows a tart wine to fit in as a balancing agent. The high acidity of a pungent Sancerre is ideal: try Lucien Crochet's *La Croix du Roy* or Cotat's *Les Culs de Beaujeu*. Though Riesling does not seem as useful, Spanish Albarino (a Riesling relative) can, in a leaner style like Morgadio, underscore the caper berry flavor while neutralizing its acidity.

# Six-Bean Salad with Horseradish, Giardiniera, and Pickled Red Onion

*I have always loved three-bean salads, but find that they are generally too bland.*
*In this version I have made the concept more interesting by adding horseradish and*
*a homemade giardiniera (which requires advance preparation).*
*This adds a beautiful zing and a perfect crunchy textural contrast to the buttery smooth beans.*
*This preparation can be served at room temperature or just slightly warm.*

**Serves 4 to 6**

*1 small red onion, thinly sliced*

*³/₄ cup Pickling Juice (see Appendices)*

*¹/₂ cup trout beans, cooked and drained*

*¹/₂ cup black calypso beans, cooked and drained*

*¹/₂ cup pinto beans, cooked and drained*

*¹/₂ cup Peruvian lima beans, cooked and drained*

*¹/₂ cup black-eyed peas, cooked and drained*

*¹/₂ cup black beans, cooked and drained*

*¹/₄ cup grated horseradish*

*1 cup Giardiniera (recipe follows)*

*2 tablespoons freshly squeezed lemon juice*

*¹/₄ cup red pearl onions, blanched and peeled*

*¹/₄ cup white pearl onions, blanched and peeled*

*Salt and pepper*

*4 teaspoons chopped flat-leaf parsley*

METHOD Place the red onion and Pickling Juice in a small saucepan. Bring to a simmer for 3 to 4 minutes and let cool. Mix all of the beans, 3 tablespoons of the horseradish, the Giardiniera, lemon juice, red onion, and red and white pearl onions in a medium bowl and season to taste with salt and pepper.

ASSEMBLY Place some of the bean mixture on each plate and top with the parsley and the remaining tablespoon of horseradish. Spoon the remaining juices from the bean mixture in the bowl around the beans and top with freshly ground black pepper.

## Giardiniera

Yield: about 4 cups

*¹/₄ cup green olives, pitted*

*¹/₄ cup sliced celery*

*¹/₄ cup diced carrot*

*¹/₄ cup diced red pepper*

*¹/₄ cup diced yellow pepper*

*¹/₄ cup sliced jalapeño pepper*

*2 tablespoons chopped flat-leaf parsley*

*1¹/₄ cups Pickling Juice (see Appendices)*

*1 teaspoon mustard seed*

*1 teaspoon black peppercorns*

*2 whole cloves*

*¹/₃ cup olive oil*

METHOD Place all of the vegetables and the parsley in a jar that has a tight fitting lid. Bring the Pickling Juice to a boil, remove from heat, and strain. Place the spices in a piece of cheesecloth and wrap up to make a sachet. Pour the Pickling Juice over the vegetables and the sachet. Let sit uncovered until cool. Top with the olive oil and cover with the tight-fitting lid. Store in the refrigerator for 2 weeks before opening. Keep refrigerated until ready to use.

### Wine Notes

This Hoppin' John relative needs a wine with intense fruit and full body along with acidity to resolve the tart vinegar element and the heat of horseradish. Prager Riesling *Steinriegl* Smaragd from Weissenkirchen, Austria, possesses all of these virtues and is a complete, delicious match. Both the 1993 and 1994 are fabulous in their youth and promise to remain intense and satisfying for many years.

# Chocolate–Bing Cherry Bread Pudding
## with White Chocolate Sorbet

*A special pastry god must have come up with the idea of pairing bittersweet chocolate and cherries.*
*The elegant flavor of good bittersweet chocolate combined with the sweet, fruity,*
*yet slightly tart cherries becomes even more incredible when served hot, as in this bread pudding.*
*The white chocolate sorbet adds the perfect delicately sweet accent.*

**Serves 4 to 6**

*1 cup Bing cherry juice*

*³/₄ cup Anglaise Sauce (see Appendices)*

*³/₄ cup heavy cream*

*¹/₄ cup plus 4 teaspoons sugar*

*2 eggs*

*6 ounces multigrain bread, cut into*
*¹/₂-inch cubes*

*1 cup chopped bittersweet chocolate*

*2 cups Bing cherries, pitted and cut*
*into quarters*

*White Chocolate Sorbet (recipe follows)*

METHOD Place the cherry juice in a small saucepan and simmer over medium heat for 10 to 15 minutes, or until reduced by half. Strain through a fine-mesh sieve and set aside. Place the Anglaise Sauce, heavy cream, sugar, and eggs in a large bowl and whisk until smooth. Add the bread, gently toss together, and let sit for 3 hours, or until most of the cream is absorbed by the bread. Fold in the chocolate and 1¹/₂ cups of the cherries. Firmly pack the mixture into four 2-inch ring molds and place on a parchment-lined sheet pan. Bake at 375 degrees for 20 to 25 minutes, or until light golden brown. Let sit for 5 minutes, then run a knife around the edges of the pudding and remove the molds. Place the remaining cherries in a small saucepan with the cherry juice and warm over medium heat just until hot.

ASSEMBLY Place one of the bread puddings in the center of each plate. Spoon some of the cherry juice and cherries around the plate and top with a scoop of the White Chocolate Sorbet.

### White Chocolate Sorbet

Yield: about 2¹/₂ cups

*7 ounces white chocolate, coarsely chopped*

*¹/₃ cup glucose*

*1 cup warm water*

METHOD Melt the white chocolate and glucose in a double boiler, stirring until smooth. Whisk in the water, remove from heat and let cool. Freeze in an ice cream machine, and keep frozen until ready to use.

### Wine Notes

This dessert is very sweet and rich, with the chocolate demanding a full, almost syrupy wine to match it. Port seems appropriate initially, yet it is not nearly sweet enough, though the berry flavors of a young Quinta connect well with the cherry element. Most impressive is a rich creamy Sherry, like the Lustau "Superior" Solera Cream. With a high proportion of Pedro Ximénez grapes, sweet sherry adds a raisiny, viscous dimension to this sweet plate.

*Experiencing a great wine tells us not only that God loves us, but that He is*

*particularly into red Burgundy.* RANDALL GRAHM, BONNY DOON VINEYARDS

In **September**, we distinctly turn the corner into the next season. For the most part, this sparks the renewal of a more serious appetite. There is, at last, a reprieve from the prolonged heat as crisper air and cooler nights accelerate the summer's more measured pace. ❧ It's a perfect climate for buttery Irish Cobbler Potatoes and summer truffles debut in time to spruce up fall dinners. Wild rice, served simply in a flavorful broth, seduces with its toothsome nuttiness. The unusual lamb's quarters lettuce makes for a great salad with a little blue cheese and the first of the season's pears. White corn, sweet, elegant, and very refined, is at once redolent of summer and hearty enough for fall appetites. Quince are converted into excellent sauces for desserts, and the tart friar and rosemary plums from Michigan are transformed into roasted fruit desserts, possibly topped with an exotic ice cream or sorbet. Such glorious foods can only signal an auspicious beginning for fall.

# Chilled Yellow Taxi Tomato Soup with Avocado-Coriander Sorbet

*As this month gives us our first night's chill, it also provides the last splendor
of summer and its warmth. There are still a few last opportunities to serve a refreshing chilled course.
With this yellow heirloom tomato version I will not go gently into those fall months.
So I emphasize my point with a scoop of icy avocado-coriander sorbet, just to make sure the soup stays good
and cold. Tomatillo, avocado, and tomato are added for texture and truly make this dish sing.*

**Serves 4**

*1 Spanish onion, diced*

*2 tablespoons olive oil*

*3 yellow heirloom tomatoes (such as
Yellow Taxi), chopped*

*Salt and pepper*

*1 avocado, peeled and pitted*

*Juice of 1 lime*

*2 tablespoons Simple Syrup
(see Appendices)*

*1 cup water*

*¼ cup chopped fresh coriander*

*4 tablespoons diced red heirloom tomato*

*4 teaspoons diced tomatillo*

*¼ cup miniature yellow tomatoes, cut in half*

*6 teaspoons Coriander Oil (see Appendices)*

*4 teaspoons julienned fresh coriander*

METHOD Sweat the onion and olive oil in a medium sauté pan over medium heat for 4 to 5 minutes, or until translucent. Add the chopped yellow tomatoes and continue to cook for 20 minutes, or until most of the liquid has been cooked out of the tomatoes. Place in a blender and purée until smooth. Pass through a fine-mesh sieve and season to taste with salt and pepper. (The soup may be thinned by the addition of tomato water). Cool completely and refrigerate until needed.

Place the avocado, lime juice, Simple Syrup, water, and chopped coriander in the blender and purée until smooth. Season to taste with salt and pepper and freeze in an ice cream machine. Keep frozen until ready to use.

Place the diced tomatoes, tomatillo, miniature yellow tomatoes, and Coriander Oil in a small bowl. Toss together and season to taste with salt and pepper.

ASSEMBLY Ladle some of the cold tomato soup into each chilled bowl. Spoon the chopped tomato mixture around the bowl and place a quenelle of the avocado sorbet in the center of the soup. Sprinkle with the julienned coriander and top with freshly ground black pepper.

## Wine Notes

This wine-friendly soup's smooth texture is balanced by the crisp refreshment of a melony Sauvignon Blanc. Spottswoode Sauvignon Blanc from the Napa Valley provides appropriate fruit and acidity for the soup and its garnishes, and enough herbal zing to meet the coriander influence. Other crisp, tart wines that succeed are Austrian Riesling (very dry) and even Greco di Tufo by Mastroberardino in Campania. Wines from Friuli or the Loire Valley are generally too austere.

# Wild Rice with Spinach, Brussels Sprouts, Cipolline Onions, and Herb Infused–Caramelized Onion Broth

*This preparation is hearty without being heavy. Another grain, or even pasta, could be easily substituted for the wild rice with equally satisfactory results. This dish would also work quite nicely with a piece of poached chicken breast or seared salmon.*

**Serves 4**

*4 Spanish onions, julienned*

*5 tablespoons butter*

*8 cups water*

*Salt and pepper*

*3 tablespoons fresh basil*

*3 tablespoons fresh chives*

*3 tablespoons fresh tarragon*

*3 tablespoons fresh flat-leaf parsley*

*8 cipolline onions, roasted, peeled, and cut into quarters*

*12 brussels sprouts, steamed and sliced into thirds*

*1 shallot, diced*

*1 bunch spinach (about 1 pound), cleaned*

*1 cup cooked wild rice*

METHOD In a large saucepan, sauté the julienned onions in 4 tablespoons of the butter over medium heat for about 30 to 40 minutes, or until caramelized. Add the water and simmer for 45 minutes. Strain through a fine-mesh sieve and return to a medium saucepan. Simmer until you have 3 cups broth and season to taste with salt and pepper.

Wrap the fresh herbs in a small piece of cheesecloth and secure to create a sachet. Place in the hot onion broth and simmer for 1 minute. Remove the sachet and discard. Place the cipolline onions and brussels sprouts in a small bowl and season to taste with salt and pepper; reheat if necessary. Place the remaining tablespoon butter and the shallot in a medium sauté pan and sweat until translucent. Add the spinach and continue to cook for 3 to 4 minutes, or until wilted. Season to taste with salt and pepper. Warm the wild rice with ¼ cup of the onion broth and season to taste with salt and pepper.

ASSEMBLY Place some of the wild rice on each plate and spread out. Place the spinach leaves at four points, meeting in the center of the plate. Arrange the brussels sprouts and cipolline onions around the rice and spoon some of the caramelized onion broth on top of the vegetables.

### Wine Notes

The toothsome heartiness of the wild rice gives the core of this preparation a nutty flavor. An oaky white wine is ideal. The New World style of Chardonnay, packed with tropical fruit, will complement the other savory flavors as well. Matanzas Creek Chardonnay Sonoma Valley is a consistent performer in every vintage; one could also imagine the extreme style of a Nautilus or Kumeu River Chardonnay from New Zealand, or perhaps a more moderate Australian Chardonnay like Coldstream Hills.

# Red and Green Pear Salad
## with Belgian Endive, Lamb's Quarters, Blue Goat Cheese, and Sherry Wine Vinaigrette

*This is the raw ingredient version of the braised endive–blue cheese dish from the January chapter.*
*It plays with the same idea, but suits the needs and appetites of early fall.*
*Perfectly ripe pears, cut up at the last moment and tossed with full-flavored cheese, sharp greens,*
*and some kind of nut element always make for a winning combination.*

### Serves 4

*1 shallot, peeled and finely diced*

*1½ tablespoons sherry wine vinegar*

*6 tablespoons olive oil*

*Salt and pepper*

*1 red pear, sliced vertically into thin slices the shape of the pear*

*1 green pear, sliced vertically into thin slices the shape of the pear*

*1½ heads Belgian endive, julienned*

*2 cups lamb's quarters greens*

*¼ pound blue goat cheese (such as Neals Yard Harbourne Blue Raw Goat's Milk), broken into chunks*

*½ cup cashews, toasted and split in half*

METHOD  Place the shallot and vinegar in a small bowl. Slowly whisk in the olive oil and season to taste with salt and pepper.

Place the pear slices, endive, lamb's quarters greens, blue goat cheese, and cashews in a large mixing bowl. Toss with 5 tablespoons of the vinaigrette and season to taste with salt and pepper.

ASSEMBLY  Place some of the pear mixture in the center of each plate and spoon the remaining vinaigrette around the salad. Top with freshly ground black pepper

### Wine Notes

This late-summer version of the salad presented in January seems more hearty and flavorful and requires a powerful, aromatic, full wine. Caymus *Conundrum* is all of these, adding intense fruit and slight wood tones to those already in the salad. It plays well with the richness of the cashews and the piquancy of the blue goat cheese while underscoring the richness of sweet fruit flavor.

# Irish Cobbler Potato Tart with Caramelized Onions, Early Winter Truffles, and Beef Stock Reduction

*As the weather begins to turn cooler, my mind turns to potatoes.*
*Here, in a tart, with early winter truffles and a little meat stock reduction, this potato dish*
*pulls us into fall. The Irish Cobbler potato is truly spectacular in its luscious creaminess,*
*and indeed almost melts into a purée as it is baked inside the layers of pastry.*
*The early winter truffles tease just enough to cause craving for their pungent winter cousin,*
*and caramelized onions add a refined, soft sweetness.*

**Serves 4**

*1 tablespoon butter*

*1 small Spanish onion, peeled and julienned*

*6 to 8 small Irish Cobbler potatoes*

*3 tablespoons heavy cream*

*Salt and pepper*

*Tart Dough (recipe follows)*

*3 early winter truffles, thinly sliced*

*1 egg yolk*

*1 tablespoon water*

*⅓ cup Beef Stock Reduction
(see Appendices)*

*4 sprigs fresh thyme*

*4 teaspoons white truffle oil*

METHOD  Sauté the butter and onions in a medium sauté pan for 10 to 15 minutes, or until caramelized and deep golden brown. Remove from the pan and cool. Slice the potatoes into ⅛-inch-thick slices, place in a bowl, and toss with the heavy cream. Season to taste with salt and pepper.

On a lightly floured surface roll out the Tart Dough ⅛ inch thick. Cut into 8 circles large enough to line and cover four 3 by ½-inch ring molds. (Other molds of a similar size will also work.) Place the ring molds on a parchment-lined sheet pan and fill with the Tart Dough, allowing for some overhang. Place a few truffle slices in the bottom of the dough and line with some of the caramelized onions. Arrange 4 or 5 potato slices in a pinwheel pattern and season with salt and pepper. Cover the potato with some of the sliced truffles and place another layer of potatoes on top. Season with salt and pepper. Place a final layer of truffles on top of the potatoes, reserving some for garnish, and spread some of the remaining caramelized onions on top. Lay another circle of tart dough on top of the onions and seal the edges. Repeat for the other 3 molds. Place in the refrigerator for 30 minutes. In a small bowl, whisk the yolk and water together. Using a pastry brush, lightly coat the top of the tart with the egg wash. Place in the oven at 375 degrees for 35 to 40 minutes, or until golden brown. Let sit for 5 minutes, remove from the rings, and cut into thirds. Place the Beef Stock Reduction in a small saucepan and warm over medium heat.

ASSEMBLY  Place three of the tart wedges on each plate with the points facing out. Spoon the Beef Stock Reduction around the tart and sprinkle with the remaining truffle slices and fresh thyme. Drizzle the white truffle oil around the plate.

## Tart Dough

*1½ cups flour*

*1 teaspoon kosher salt*

*1 cup cold butter, chopped*

*⅓ cup ice water*

METHOD  Place the flour, salt, and butter in a bowl and, using a fork or dough cutter, cut the butter into the flour until you have pea-size chunks. Add the water and mix until just combined (the dough should have visible pieces of butter). Form into a ball, wrap in plastic, and place in the refrigerator for 1 hour before rolling out.

## Wine Notes

The meat element nudges this tart to become a red wine dish, though a delicate red, preferably one with some age and secondary aromas and with little tannin, is best. A few mature Pinot Noirs stand out: Eyrie Pinot Noir Reserve Willamette Valley 1988; Vosne Romanee Henri Jayer 1986; Mazis-Chambertin Faiveley 1978. Their delicacy and mature sweetness merge well with the truffle and onion influences. And they offer a bouillon aroma found only in an older wine. Other options include older Rioja in the traditional style of La Rioja Alta *Reserva 904* 1981 or Muga's *Prado Enea* 1982. If you opt for a vegetarian sauce, select a white wine from the Rhône, such as mature Hermitage Blanc (Chave's 1988 is fine) or an older Meursault.

# White Corn Pancakes with Faux Foie Gras and Apple Juice Reduction

*When chef Norman Van Aken first served me and my wife, Lynn, his
Down Island French Toast, which is layers of seared foie gras, vanilla, and pepper-spiked brioche,
sauced and enhanced with tropical fruit essences, it was so phenomenal that
Lynn ordered another—seven courses later—for dessert!
This preparation is a tribute to his wizardry and genius and can be served
either as a playful first course or as a breakfast dish.*

**Serves 4**

*2 shallots, peeled and minced*

*5 tablespoons butter*

*2¹/₂ cups white corn kernels*

*Salt and pepper*

*2 cups apple juice*

*2 tablespoons flat-leaf parsley, chopped*

*2 tablespoons lukewarm water*

*³/₄ teaspoon active dry yeast*

*1 cup milk*

*1 teaspoon rice vinegar*

*1 egg*

*¹/₄ cup melted butter, cooled*

*1 cup flour*

*3 tablespoons chopped fresh chives*

*1 quince, peeled and chopped*

*3 French butter or Bosc pears*

*2 teaspoons grapeseed oil*

METHOD Sweat the shallots with 2 tablespoons of the butter in a medium sauté pan until translucent. Add the corn and continue to cook for 10 to 12 minutes, or until the corn is tender. Season to taste with salt and pepper and allow to cool. Place the apple juice in a small saucepan and bring to a simmer for 35 to 45 minutes, or until reduced to 1 cup. Whisk in 3 tablespoons butter and add ³/₄ cups of the cooled corn and the parsley.

Place the lukewarm water and yeast in a small bowl and let stand for 3 minutes. Place the milk, vinegar, egg, melted butter, and the yeast mixture in a medium bowl and whisk together until combined. Add the flour, chives, and the remaining 1³/₄ cups white corn and season with salt and pepper. Place the quince in a small saucepan and cover with water. Simmer over medium heat for 15 to 20 minutes, or until the quince is soft. Place in a blender and purée until smooth. Slice the pears into twelve ¹/₄-inch-thick whole slices, keeping the skin on. Place the pears and the grapeseed oil in a large sauté pan and cook over medium-high heat until caramelized on each side. Spoon 2 tablespoons of the corn batter in a nonstick sauté pan (oil is unnecessary) for each pancake. Cook for 3 to 4 minutes, or until golden brown on each side. Continue this process until you have 16 pancakes. Cut the pancakes into squares and keep warm.

ASSEMBLY Place one of the pear slices in the center of each plate, spoon some of the corn-apple sauce over the pear, and stagger two of the pancakes on top of the pear. Place a dollop of quince on top of the pancakes and continue the layering process until you have 3 layers of pear and 2 layers of pancakes. Spoon some of the remaining sauce around the plate.

## Wine Notes

The sweetness of this dish requires some sweetness in the accompanying wine, though not at the residual sugar level of a dessert wine. Though Riesling seems a likely candidate because of its applelike nose, this characteristic seems to cancel out the dominant apple flavor of the dish. More harmonizing, especially for the white corn's sweetness, is the style of a Pinot Gris *vendange tardive* from Alsace. The *Clos Jebsal* Pinot Gris VT by Zind Humbrecht is a resplendent wine of sweetness and balance, and, incidentally, is also a fantastic foie gras wine.

# Oven-Roasted Rosemary Plums with Friar Plum Sauce and Black Sesame Seed Brittle Ice Cream

*I am especially fond of whole roasted fruit stuffed with some dried fruit and roasted nuts and served warm with ice cream. When fall plums come along, they are superb for this composition. They are slightly tarter than the summer varieties, which make them better for pairing with a rich ice cream and the concentrated full flavor of dried fruit. Here the accompanying Friar plum sauce is not exactly sweet, and thus benefits tremendously from a little of the black sesame seed syrup drizzled around the edges. The sesame and plum combination is a melding of two flavors that really complement each other fantastically.*

**Serves 4**

*4 Friar plums, peeled and pitted*
*1 cup water*
*4 Rosemary plums, peeled*
*1 cup Simple Syrup (see Appendices)*
*1/3 cup pecans*
*1 tablespoon black sesame seeds*
*2 tablespoons dried black currants*
*1/2 cup dried apple, cut into small dice*
*2 tablespoons Preserved Ginger (see Appendices)*
*Black Sesame Seed Brittle Ice Cream (recipe follows)*
*1 1/2 teaspoons tiny mint leaves*

METHOD  Coarsely chop one of the Friar plums and place in a small saucepan with 1/2 cup of the water. Simmer for 15 to 20 minutes, or until most of the liquid is evaporated. Place in a blender and purée until smooth. Cut the remaining 3 Friar plums into 1/2-inch wedges, and place on a nonstick sheet pan. Bake at 275 degrees for 1 1/2 hours, or until dry to the touch (they will still be moist in the middle but the outer portion will appear dry).

Slice the top off the Rosemary plums, and reserve. Using a paring knife, remove the pit and hollow out about one-third of the center of the plums, keeping them whole. Place the tops back on the plums and place in an ovenproof pan with the remaining 1/2 cup water. Bake at 350 degrees for 1 1/2 hours, or until extremely tender (remove the tops after 45 minutes so they do not turn mushy). Place the Simple Syrup in a small saucepan over medium heat and sim-mer for 5 to 7 minutes, or until reduced by one-third. Cool and store in the refrigerator.

Toss the pecans with 6 tablespoons of the reduced Simple Syrup and place on a nonstick sheet pan. Bake at 350 degrees for 12 to 15 minutes, or until the syrup has dried and crystallized on the pecans (turn the pecans with a spatula every 5 to 7 minutes to redistribute the syrup). Remove the pecans from the oven, cool, and coarsely chop. Place the remaining 5 tablespoons of the reduced Simple Syrup in a small cup and stir in the sesame seeds. Place the pecans, black currants, dried apple, Preserved Ginger, dried plum pieces, and 3 tablespoons of the sesame seed syrup in a small bowl and toss together. Fill each of the plums with the mixture. Bake at 350 degrees for 5 minutes, or until warm in the center.

ASSEMBLY  Place some of the puréed plum in the center of each plate. Set one whole roasted plum in the center of the sauce. Drizzle a few teaspoons of the sesame seed syrup around the outer portion of the plum. Place a small scoop of the Black Sesame Seed Brittle Ice Cream on top of the plum and set the top of the plum against the ice cream. Garnish with a few tiny mint leaves.

## Black Sesame Seed Brittle Ice Cream

Yield: 1 quart

*1 1/2 cups heavy cream*
*3/4 cup half-and-half*
*3/4 cup milk*
*6 egg yolks*
*1 3/4 cups sugar*
*1/4 cup black sesame seeds*

METHOD  Heat the cream, half-and-half, and milk in a medium saucepan over medium heat until it simmers. Place the yolks in a bowl and whisk in 3/4 cup of the sugar. Slowly whisk in the hot cream mixture and return to the saucepan. Over medium heat, stir constantly for 2 minutes, or until the mixture coats the back of a spoon. Strain through a fine-mesh sieve and cool completely. Place the remaining 1 cup sugar in a nonstick pan and, over medium-low heat, slowly caramelize the sugar. Once the sugar is completely melted and golden brown, stir in the sesame seeds. Pour the mixture onto a nonstick sheet pan and let set. Once hard, break up the brittle and place in a blender or food processor and process until it is finely ground. Fold into the ice cream base and freeze in an ice cream machine. Store in the freezer until needed. (The extra ice cream will keep nicely in the freezer.)

## Wine Notes

The role of wine here—aside, of course, from being sweet—is to play with the ginger flavor and not to mask the plum's ripeness. The renaissance of Tokaji Aszu has made possible sweet, honeylike wines with the right viscosity, exotic spiciness and clean, unoxidized fruit aromas to match well with the complex elements in this dish. The Royal Tokaji Wine Co., a group of investors remaking Tokaji, have featured several single-vineyard wines in their range; we find the 5 puttonyos *Birsalma's* the most satisfying, as it retains some useful acidity and is not too unctuous.

October brings beautiful temperate days, but its brisk nights are a preview of what is to come. Indeed, we invariably experience our first freeze early in the month. But October provides much to be joyous about. ❧ It is a great time for turnips and turnip greens, red Swiss chard, and intense dandelion greens. Sweet dumpling squash makes a tremendous, sultry soup, with practically no additional ingredients. Porcini mushrooms are beautiful now, practically a song from the earth. Butternut squash and tiny beets, including the interesting candystripe beet, abound. Sage and marjoram provide the ideal accent for many fall dishes because they offer refined flavors with an element of grace and maturity. Chiles, such as poblanos, are perfect for adding a little zing. And for dessert, what could be better than a pear charlotte? As crimson and amber leaves flutter on the trees, it feels right to trade summer's abundance for fall's full flavors.

# Sweet Dumpling Squash Soup
# with Crispy Squash Pieces

*Squash or pumpkin soup tastes even better when served in its own shell as the natural flavors are enhanced. Plus, you can enjoy the added pleasure of being able to eat the pulp from the sides and, in many cases, to eat the skin as well. I really enjoy winter squash, the sweeter the better, and I find dumpling squash particularly satisfying. For an interesting textural touch, I add a few crispy squash pieces, but aside from that, this preparation is the ultimate in simplicity.*

**Serves 4**

*5 sweet dumpling squashes, tops cut off and seeds removed*

*5 teaspoons olive oil*

*Salt and pepper*

*2 tablespoons butter*

*1 small Spanish onion, chopped*

*2 cups water*

*Oven-Dried Squash Pieces (recipe follows)*

*2 teaspoons chopped chervil*

METHOD Season the inside of the squashes with olive oil, salt, and pepper. Place upside down on a sheet tray and pour ½ inch of water on the tray. Bake at 375 degrees for 1 hour, or until the squashes are tender. Remove from the oven and completely scrape out the pulp of 1 squash, discarding the skin. Scrape the pulp out of the remaining four squashes, leaving ¼ inch of the flesh adhered to the skin. Sweat the butter and onion in a small sauté pan over medium heat until translucent. Place the onion, water, and squash pulp in a blender and purée until smooth. Pass through a fine-mesh sieve, and reheat in a small saucepan. Season to taste with salt and pepper.

Place the squashes in the oven at 350 degrees for 5 minutes. Remove and fill with the hot soup.

ASSEMBLY Place one of the squashes in the center of each plate. Place a few of the Oven-Dried Squash Pieces on top of the soup and arrange some around the plate. Sprinkle with the chopped chervil.

## Oven-Dried Squash Pieces

Yield: 1½ cups

*1 small sweet dumpling squash, cut into quarters and seeds removed*

*Salt*

METHOD Using a mandoline or a knife, cut squash into paper-thin slices. Lay flat on a nonstick sheet pan and lightly season with salt. Place in the oven at 275 degrees for 20 to 30 minutes, or until golden brown and dry to the touch. (Watch carefully as they can burn easily). Remove from sheet pan and let cool. The squash pieces should be crispy once cool. If they are not, return them to the oven for a few more minutes. Store until use in an airtight container at room temperature.

### Wine Notes

The squash is so sweet that only a very rich, buttery Chardonnay will match its intensity. Mer et Soleil, a ripe, round Chardonnay from the Central Coast, made by Chuck Wagner of Caymus, is exceptionally well-suited to the dish. This wine's oakiness only adds to the richness of the soup and is texturally lush enough for the creaminess of the roasted squash. Chervil and parsley accent rather than block a rich wine's effect.

# Roasted White Beet Salad with Gala Apples, Dandelion Greens, and Roasted Poblano Chile Vinaigrette

*This is a very refreshing salad with several different textures and disparate flavors melding into a cohesive blend. Tart, crispy apple pieces; soft, sweet roasted white beets; bitter, crunchy dandelion greens; playfully spicy poblano vinaigrette; and rich pistachios combine for a stunning effect. This dish would work perfectly by itself, before a main entrée, or even as a first course before a rich game bird.*

**Serves 4**

*1 large white beet*

*1 shallot, peeled*

*6 tablespoons olive oil*

*1 large poblano chile, roasted, skinned and seeded*

*2 tablespoons water*

*Salt and pepper*

*1 tablespoon rice vinegar*

*20 dandelion greens*

*1 small Gala apple, julienned*

*¼ cup pistachios, toasted and coarsely chopped*

METHOD Roast the beet at 375 degrees for 2 to 2½ hours, or until tender. Remove from the oven and let cool. Peel the skin, removing the brown outer portion. Cut the peeled beet into batons and set aside.

Place the shallot and 3 tablespoons of the olive oil in a small ovenproof pan and bake at 375 degrees for 30 minutes, or until tender. Remove from the pan and reserve the olive oil. Remove the tough outer layer of the shallot and cut into thin pieces. Coarsely chop half of the roasted chile and place it in the blender with the reserved oil the shallots were cooked in and the water. Purée until smooth, then strain through a fine-mesh sieve. Season to taste with salt and pepper and store in the refrigerator until needed.

Cut the remaining chile into small dice and place in a small bowl with the vinegar. Slowly whisk in the remaining 3 tablespoons olive oil and season to taste with salt and pepper. Lightly toss the dandelion greens, shallot, white beets, and apple with the vinaigrette and season to taste with salt and pepper.

ASSEMBLY Place 5 of the dandelion greens on each plate. Arrange the apple, beet, and shallot mixture on top of the greens and place the pistachios around the greens. Spoon the chile purée on top of and around the salad, and finish with freshly ground black pepper.

## Wine Notes

Here Sauvignon Blanc–based wines will shine, whether French or American. The white beet is not nearly as sweet as a red beet would be, and the apple suggests a lightly fruity wine with a little oak to block the fresh flavors. Pavillon Blanc du Château Margaux offers a rare style of Sauvignon Blanc with subtle oak influences; it is crisp enough, but not austere—a fine match for the radish flavor.

# White Corn Grits with Turnip Confit and Beef Stock Broth

*Grits are among the most soul-satisfying foods I know. They have a creaminess and a delicacy, but at the same time they stand up to, and indeed show off, any strong or assertive flavors while still keeping their own identity. This simple preparation with turnips, the last of the season's sweet corn, and a light meat broth is a great segue into colder weather dishes.*

**Serves 4**

*1 small turnip, peeled and cut in half*

*2 sprigs thyme*

*³/4 cup plus 3 tablespoons butter*

*Salt and pepper*

*3 cups turnip greens, stems removed*

*6 green onions, blanched and sliced into ¹/4-inch pieces on the bias*

*¹/2 cup corn kernels, cooked*

*1¹/2 cups cooked white corn grits*

*1 cup porcini mushrooms, roasted and cut into small wedges*

*4 sage leaves, fried in grapeseed oil*

*2 cups Beef Stock Broth (recipe follows)*

*4 teaspoons chervil sprigs*

METHOD  Place the turnip halves, thyme sprigs and ¹/2 cup of the butter in a medium saucepan, cover with water, and season with salt and pepper. Simmer over medium-low heat for 40 to 50 minutes, or until tender. Remove from heat, cut into batons, and store in the cooking liquid until needed.

Coarsely chop the turnip greens and place in a sauté pan with 1 tablespoon of the butter. Sauté over medium-high heat for 2 to 3 minutes, or until wilted. Season to taste with salt and pepper. Place the green onions into a medium sauté pan with 1 tablespoon of the butter and the corn. Sauté for 2 to 3 minutes and season to taste with salt and pepper. Reheat the grits (if necessary) and fold in the green onion mixture and half of the turnip greens. Season to taste with salt and pepper. Place the mushrooms in a small sauté pan with the remaining 1 tablespoon of butter and sauté over medium heat until the mushrooms are lightly caramelized. Season to taste with salt and pepper.

ASSEMBLY  Place a 2- to 3-inch ring mold in the center of each plate and fill with the grit mixture. Insert one of the fried sage leaves into the center of the timbale, remove the mold, and spoon some of the Beef Stock Broth around the plate. Arrange the remaining turnip greens around the timbale, along with the mushrooms and chervil.

## Beef Stock Broth

Yield: about 2 cups

*5 pounds beef bones*

*1 carrot, chopped*

*1 stalk celery, chopped*

*1 yellow onion, chopped*

*1 leek, chopped*

*¹/2 head of garlic, cut in half*

*1 tablespoon grapeseed oil*

*¹/4 cup tomato concassée*

*2 cups red wine*

METHOD  Place the bones in a roasting pan and bake at 450 degrees for 1 to 2 hours, or until golden brown. Caramelize the carrot, celery, onion, leek, and garlic with the grapeseed oil in a large stockpot. Add the tomato concassée and continue to cook for 5 minutes. Deglaze with the red wine and reduce for 15 minutes, or until most of the wine is cooked out. Add the browned bones and cover with cold water. Bring to a boil and simmer over medium heat for 8 hours. Strain through a fine-mesh sieve and slowly cook over medium heat until reduced to about 2 cups of stock.

## Wine Notes

The turnip greens and the turnip confit itself require a more intense, even somewhat tannic, wine. With meat stock as a saucing influence, the wine choice could be a medium-weight red, such as the Saint Joseph by Roger Blachon or a young Carneros Pinot Noir like Domaine Carneros. The grits become the anchor for the flavors of the dish, though they are not an eminent flavor contributor, and the porcini mushroom presence also begs for a lightish red.

# Fingerling Potatoes, Napa Cabbage, and Root Vegetables with Golden Beet Stock and Marjoram

*This combination is as hearty as a stew yet it is also quite light.*
*The cabbage provides just the right crunchiness, the potatoes, a satiny creaminess,*
*and the root vegetables, a wonderful range of flavors.*
*Golden beet stock and fresh marjoram add textural flavor accents that help elevate*
*this dish to pure elegant refinement in spite of its rustic appearance.*

**Serves 4**

*½ cup diced carrots*

*½ cup diced turnips*

*½ cup diced red beets*

*½ cup diced golden beets*

*½ cup diced candystripe beets*

*2 shallots, chopped*

*½ cup peeled and chopped carrots*

*½ cup peeled and chopped turnips*

*1 tablespoon grapeseed oil*

*1 cup peeled and chopped golden beets*

*8 cups water*

*Salt and pepper*

*16 small white pearl onions, peeled*

*1 tablespoon olive oil*

*28 small fingerling potatoes, boiled and peeled*

*1½ cups napa cabbage, cut into thick chiffonade*

*4 tablespoons Basil Oil (see Appendices)*

*4 teaspoons fresh marjoram leaves*

METHOD In a small saucepan, blanch the diced vegetables separately until tender. Shock in ice water, drain, and set aside. Lightly caramelize the shallot, carrots, and turnips in the grapeseed oil over medium-high heat. Add the chopped golden beets and water and simmer for 1 hour. Strain through a fine-mesh sieve, return to the heat, and simmer for 15 minutes, or until reduced to 3 cups. Season to taste with salt and pepper.

Toss the pearl onions with the olive oil and roast at 375 degrees for 10 to 15 minutes. Remove from the pan and season with salt and pepper. Just prior to assembly, reheat the potatoes, diced vegetables, and pearl onions in the beet stock. Remove from heat and add the napa cabbage.

ASSEMBLY Arrange the diced vegetables, potatoes, and pearl onions in each bowl. Spoon in the beet stock and drizzle the Basil Oil around the bowl. Top with the marjoram and freshly ground black pepper.

**Wine Notes**

Here is a complex dish matched by a firm, dry Riesling or Pinot Gris. The many top vineyard sites (Ried Achleiten, Ried Klaus) of Prager in the Wachau provide great dry Riesling matches, and the Kuentz-Bas Tokay-Pinot Gris of Alsace is friendly. A completely different approach is the fine dry Italian whites from Campania, like Greco di Tufo Mastroberardino. All these wines are slightly earthy, yet with pure fruit expression. They meet well with the overtly earthy potato flavor and add firmness to the beet stock.

# Rice Beans and Matsutake Mushrooms Wrapped in Red Swiss Chard with Garlic-Mushroom Broth and Tarragon

~~~~~~~~~~~~~~~~~~~~~~~~~~~~~~~~~~~~~~~~~~~~~~~~~

*I love little packages. They are easy to make ahead and can contain anything your imagination desires.*
*Here I paired meltaway rice beans with pungent, sensual, matsutake mushrooms.*
*This dish is very simple and incredibly flavorful. The elegance of tarragon adds the perfect*
*refined flavor, and the chard adds just the right playful edge.*

**Serves 4**

*5 tablespoons butter*

*1 cup small-diced carrots*

*Salt and pepper*

*1¹/₂ cups cooked rice beans*

*2 cups matsutake mushrooms, roasted (see Appendices) and cut into small wedges*

*3 tablespoons chopped chives*

*4 large red Swiss chard leaves, blanched and shocked*

*4 teaspoons Swiss Chard Oil (recipe follows)*

*1 cup Garlic-Mushroom Broth (recipe follows)*

*3 teaspoons tarragon leaves*

*4 teaspoons Tarragon Oil (see Appendices)*

METHOD Place 2 teaspoons of the butter and the carrots in a small sauté pan and quickly sauté over medium heat until just golden brown. Remove from heat and season to taste with salt and pepper. Warm the rice beans, ¹/₂ cup of the carrots, and 1 cup of the mushrooms in a small saucepan over medium heat. Fold in the chives and season to taste with salt and pepper.

Lay the Swiss chard leaves flat and, using a knife, remove the thick inner spine of the chard, leaving the leaf in one piece. Lightly brush the outer side of the leaves with the Swiss Chard Oil and season the inner side with salt and pepper. Spoon ¹/₂ cup of the rice-bean mixture in the middle of the Swiss chard leaf and carefully roll up, fold-ing the sides in, to create a shape similar to a thick cigar. Bake at 350 degrees for 3 to 5 minutes, or until just warm, and cut in half.

Quickly sauté the remaining mushrooms with 1 teaspoon of the butter. Quickly sauté and season to taste with salt and pepper. Warm the Garlic-Mushroom Broth in a small saucepan, slowly whisk in the remaining butter, and season to taste with salt and pepper.

ASSEMBLY Place the two halves of the Swiss chard rolls side by side in the center of each plate. Arrange the remaining mushrooms and carrots around the rolls and spoon the Garlic-Mushroom Broth around the plate. Place a few tarragon leaves around the plate and drizzle with the Tarragon Oil.

## Garlic-Mushroom Broth

Yield: 1 cup

*8 ounces cremini mushrooms, chopped*

*4 ounces portobello mushrooms, chopped*

*8 ounces button mushrooms, chopped*

*3 cloves garlic, chopped*

*2 cloves garlic, whole*

*2 tablespoons olive oil*

*Salt and pepper*

*6 cups water*

METHOD Sauté the mushrooms, garlic, and olive oil in a medium saucepan over medium-high heat for 5 to 7 minutes.

Season with salt and pepper. Add the water and simmer for 1 hour. Strain through a fine-mesh sieve and return to the stove. Continue to simmer until it is reduced to 1 cup of broth.

## Swiss Chard Oil

Yield: about 1 cup

*2 large leaves Swiss chard*

*¹/₂ cup grapeseed oil*

*¹/₂ cup olive oil*

METHOD Place the Swiss chard in boiling salted water for 15 seconds, quickly remove, and shock in ice water. Drain and squeeze out all of the excess liquid. Coarsely chop the Swiss chard and place in the blender with the oil. Purée for about 3 minutes, or until smooth and bright green. Refrigerate for 1 day. Strain through a fine-mesh sieve, refrigerate 1 more day, and decant.

## Wine Notes

The chard gives a faint impression of anise in this arrangement, suggesting Rhône varieties such as Marsanne and Roussanne. But the wines of the Rhône seem too hard for the rich mushroom flavor and the creamy beans. New World versions are more successful: Bonny Doon *Le Sophiste* and Qupé Marsanne are full-bodied and rich flavored enough for the rich elements of the dish, while marrying well with the mushroom broth.

# Maytag Blue Cheese Soufflé with Dried-Fig Brioche, Black Corinth Grapes, and Muscat Grape Reduction

*This is a lighter way to enjoy a spectacular cheese. Served on a small piece of crispy brioche
and drizzled with Muscat grape reduction, this is the perfect transition course from entrée to dessert.
As a delicate, warm appetizer, it could also be a great way to start a meal.
The marriage between the creamy blue cheese with just the right amount of intensity,
and the sweet yet slightly acidic grape sauce, is virtually seamless.*

**Serves 4 to 6**

*3 cups Muscat grapes*

*½ cup water*

*½ cup milk*

*2 tablespoons plus 1 teaspoon butter*

*⅓ cup flour*

*2 egg yolks*

*¼ cup egg whites (about 3 to 4 whites)*

*4 ounces Maytag blue cheese, broken
into chunks*

*3 tablespoons finely chopped black walnuts*

*4 slices Dried-Fig Brioche (recipe follows)*

*1 cup Black Corinth grapes*

METHOD  Place the Muscat grapes and water in a small saucepan and simmer for 30 minutes. Pass through a fine-mesh sieve, squeezing all the juice out of the grapes. Place the juice in a small saucepan and simmer for 10 minutes, or until reduced to about ½ cup of juice.

Place the milk and 2 tablespoons of the butter in a small saucepan and bring to a boil. Stir in the flour and return to a boil. Place the mixture in a large bowl, whisk vigorously to eliminate any steam, then fold in the egg yolks. In a separate bowl, whip the egg whites to stiff peaks. Break one-half of the blue cheese into small pieces and fold into the soufflé base in the saucepan. Using your hands or a spatula, gently fold in the egg whites. Butter 4 to 6 small (1½-inch-high by 1-inch-wide) timbale molds (other molds of similar size will also work), and line them with chopped walnuts. Spoon in the soufflé batter. Place in a water bath and bake at 400 degrees for 30 minutes, or until golden brown. Cut the Brioche in 4½-inch-thick squares, slightly larger than the timbale mold. Sauté the Brioche squares in the 1 remaining teaspoon of the butter until golden brown.

ASSEMBLY  Place a square of the brioche in the center of each plate and top with a soufflé. Arrange the grapes and remaining cheese around the plate. Spoon the muscat grape reduction around the soufflé.

## Dried-Fig Brioche

Yield: one 4 by 9-inch loaf

*1½ teaspoons active dry yeast*

*2 tablespoons warm water*

*2 tablespoons sugar*

*3 eggs*

*1½ teaspoons salt*

*2 cups flour*

*1 cup butter, softened*

*1½ cups dried figs, chopped*

*½ cup black walnuts, chopped*

METHOD  Butter and flour a 4 by 9-inch bread pan. Proof the yeast in the water with 1 tablespoon of the sugar. In a large bowl, whisk together the eggs, the remaining tablespoon sugar, and the salt. Add the yeast mixture and stir in the flour. Using your hands, work the butter into the dough until it is fully incorporated. Fold in the dried figs and walnuts. Place in an oiled bowl and cover with plastic wrap. Let rise in a warm place for about 2 hours, or until doubled in size. Punch down and place into the prepared bread pan. Cover and let sit in a warm place for 1 hour. Bake at 375 degrees for 30 to 40 minutes, or until golden brown. Remove from the oven and from the pan. Allow to cool completely on a wire rack.

## Wine Notes

This playful savory-sweet course relies on an extremely tart cheese and many fruit elements. Sweet wines from the Loire Valley give these same pleasures—tartness and exceptional fruit. Bonnezeaux from Château de Fesles is a remarkable wine for this combination—not too sweet, but certainly balanced, and not an overtly desserty wine. More intense is the Vouvray Moelleux by Huet from a ripe, warm vintage like 1989, offering more unctuous fruit and more sweetness. These wines age magnificently. We have served this course at Charlie Trotter's with Loire sweet wines as old as 1924!

# Pear Charlotte with Butternut Squash–Black Pepper Ice Cream and Pear-Caramel Sauce

*What I love most about this charlotte is the crispy shell.*
*The whole wheat bread, with its steaming-hot pielike pear center, is heightened by the melting*
*butternut squash ice cream, resulting in a dish whose sum is greater than the parts.*

**Serves 4**

*5 Bosc pears, peeled*
*1 1/2 cups sugar*
*3 tablespoons butter*
*1/2 cup Sauterne*
*1 stick cinnamon*
*1/4 cup Brazil nuts, toasted and chopped*
*16 thin slices whole wheat bread*
*Butternut Squash–Black Pepper Ice Cream (recipe follows)*
*4 teaspoons Brazil nuts, toasted and shaved*

**METHOD** Juice 2 of the pears and set aside. Slowly caramelize the sugar over medium-low heat in a medium saucepan. When it has turned brown, add 2 tablespoons of the butter, the pear juice, Sauterne, and cinnamon stick. Continue to cook over low heat for about 30 minutes, or until the consistency is smooth. Remove from heat and set aside. Cut 2 of the pears into medium dice, place in a small bowl, and toss with 1/4 cup of the pear-caramel sauce. Butter four 3-inch ceramic ramekins with the remaining tablespoon of butter and line them with the chopped Brazil nuts. Cut 12 pieces of the whole wheat bread into squares just as high as your molds. Brush the squares with a thick layer of the pear-caramel sauce and line the the sides of the mold overlapping

slightly. Cut 4 circles out of the remaining bread large enough to fill the bottom of the mold. Brush with the pear-caramel sauce and press into the bottom of the mold. Spoon the chopped pear mixture into each of the prepared molds and bake at 400 degrees for 30 to 40 minutes, or until the bread is crispy.

Cut the remaining pear in thin vertical slices. Sauté the slices with the remaining pear-caramel sauce over medium heat for 5 minutes, or until the pears are tender. Let sit for 3 minutes and use immediately.

**ASSEMBLY** Invert one of the pear charlottes in the center of each plate. Arrange some of the pear slices on top of the charlotte and place a quenelle of the Butternut Squash–Black Pepper Ice Cream on the pear slices. Sprinkle with the shaved nuts and spoon the sauce the pears were sautéed in around the plate.

## Butternut Squash–Black Pepper Ice Cream

Yield: 1 quart

*3/4 cup heavy cream*
*1/2 cup milk*
*1/2 cup half-and-half*
*3 egg yolks*

*3/4 cup sugar*
*3 cups baked butternut squash*
*Freshly ground black pepper*

**METHOD** Heat the heavy cream, milk, and half-and-half in a medium saucepan. Place the yolks and sugar in a medium bowl and whisk until smooth. Slowly add the hot cream mixture while constantly whisking. Return to the saucepan while continually stirring. Heat for 2 to 3 minutes, or until the mixture coats the back of a spoon. Strain through a fine-mesh sieve and cool in an ice water bath. Place the ice cream base and butternut squash in a blender and purée until smooth. Pass through a fine-mesh sieve and season to taste with freshly ground pepper. Freeze in an ice cream machine and keep frozen until ready to use.

### Wine Notes

Muscat-based dessert wines work best here because of their ability to match the sweetness of each element; their fruit style transcends the complexities of the presentation. Muskat Ottonel, Moscato Giallo di Veneto, and Muscat de Beaumes de Venise all have rich, assertive fruit, good sweetness, and appropriate viscosity for this unusual ice cream and sugary sauce.

As **November**'s nights become bracing and the days shorter, my appetite builds exponentially. Mostly, I find I desire robust and rich flavors. My cravings, though, are easily sated. ℀ I especially love hard winter squashes with their earthy complexity and lightness. I also yearn for grains like the nutty-flavored mixture known as kashi. The aristocratic salsify is perfect for a purée or in an intricate terrine preparation. Wood ear mushrooms are great for stir-fries or complexly flavored noodle dishes, like my friend Arun Sampanthavivat's Phad Thai. Mizuna and tatsoi are splendid lightly wilted in warm salads. November is the ultimate apple month, and such underrated and underused foodstuffs as dates, pomegranates, and chestnuts show their value as versatile savory-sweet accents. November sets the stage for that celebratory holiday eating, which inevitably reminds us that the best things in life involve the pleasures of the table.

# Salsify and Sweet Potato Terrine with Two Enriching Vinaigrettes

*The easy-to-make salsify terrine is the perfect way to open a special dinner party.*
*It is elegant and flavorful and it exposes people to a foodstuff that may be new for them.*
*In this terrine, two vinaigrettes add extraordinary depth of flavor. The truffle vinaigrette adds a rich*
*sensuality, and the pickled salsify vinaigrette provides just the right refined acidic accent.*

**Serves 4**

*13 (8-inch-long) stalks salsify*

*3 cups milk*

*2 cups plus 3 tablespoons water*

*Salt and pepper*

*1 sweet potato, baked and peeled*

*⅛ teaspoon gelatin*

*10 green onions, green tops only*

*Pickling Juice (see Appendices)*

*1 teaspoon rice vinegar*

*1 teaspoon sherry vinegar*

*4 tablespoons white truffle oil*

*1 small truffle, cut in small dice*

*3 tablespoons Mushroom Juice
(see Appendices)*

*4 teaspoons chervil sprigs*

*4 teaspoons Basil Oil (see Appendices)*

METHOD  Peel the salsify and place stalks in a medium saucepan with the milk and 2 cups of the water. Simmer for 15 minutes, or until tender. Remove from the liquid, let cool, then season with salt and pepper. Place the sweet potato in a small bowl, mash to a smooth pulp, and season to taste with salt and pepper.

Lightly oil the inside of a terrine mold (an 8 by 1½ by 2¼-inch terrine mold is best, but other similar-size molds will also work) and line it with plastic wrap, leaving a 2-inch overhang. Trim the salsify so they are even in thickness. Place three stalks of salsify side by side on the bottom of the mold. Using a small spatula, spread some of the sweet potato mixture on top of the salsify layer. Press down to ensure the sweet potato fills the spaces between the salsify, leaving a ¼-inch layer of sweet potato on top. Repeat this process three times, then cover with the overhanging plastic wrap. Place in the refrigerator for 1 hour before unmolding.

In the meantime, place the remaining 3 tablespoons of water in a small cup and sprinkle the gelatin on top; let it sit for 3 minutes. In a small saucepan over medium heat, slowly warm the gelatin mixture and set aside. Place the green onion tops in boiling salted water for 30 seconds, remove, and shock in ice water. Drain and pat dry. Using a paring knife, slit the green onions open and spread flat. Scrape the inside with the knife, removing the clear membrane. Spread out a large sheet of plastic wrap at least 9 by 12 inches and lay the green onion pieces on it, slightly overlapping each other with the inner side facing up. Continue the overlapping until you create a 9 by 12-inch layer. Lightly brush with the gelatin and season with salt and pepper.

Remove the terrine from the mold and carefully remove the plastic wrap. Place the terrine on the bottom edge of the green onion wrap and roll it in the wrap, pulling the plastic wrap away with each turn. Once the terrine is fully encased with the onions, cover with a fresh piece of plastic wrap and place in the refrigerator for 30 minutes before slicing.

Place the Pickling Juice in a small saucepan and bring to a simmer. Remove from heat, add the remaining salsify stalk, and let it marinate for 2 hours in the Pickling Juice; remove and cut into small dice. Place the pickled salsify in a small bowl with the two vinegars. Slowly whisk in 2 tablespoons of the white truffle oil and season to taste with salt and pepper. In a separate bowl, place the diced truffle and Mushroom Juice and slowly whisk in the remaining 2 tablespoons white truffle oil. Season to taste with salt and pepper.

Slice the terrine into ½-inch slices with the plastic wrap left on (remove the wrap before serving). Season each piece with salt and pepper and rub a dash of the salsify vinaigrette on top of the terrine.

ASSEMBLY  Place a slice of terrine in the center of each plate. Spoon some of each vinaigrette around opposite sides of the terrine, sprinkle with the chervil, and drizzle the Basil Oil around the plate.

**Wine Notes**

The full, rich taste of salsify seems heightened by a smoky aspect, suggesting this attribute in the potential wine. Full-bodied, dry, somewhat oaky wines like the Château de Beaucastel Châteauneuf-du-Pape Blanc Roussanne *Vielles Vignes* with some age will be magnificent, as the earthy aromas and full flavor of the wine matches the terrine's heartiness, which the truffle seems to enhance. We can also endorse bigger white Burgundies; the almost diesel-like style of a mature Leroy Puligny or a Jobard Meursault would also be exciting.

# Red Kuri Squash Soup with Herbed Spätzle and Curry Butter

*Red kuri squash explodes with flavor. It is also among the least starchy of the hard squashes.*
*This soup recipe is very simple and straightforward. The herbed spätzle*
*adds a delicate textural component and the drizzle of curry butter contributes the*
*perfect exotic zing and a touch of necessary richness.*

**Serves 4**

*6 cups kuri squash juice*
*5 tablespoons butter*
*Salt and pepper*
*1 small kuri squash*
*2 teaspoons olive oil*
*1 egg*
*⅓ cup milk*
*1 cup flour*
*2 tablespoons chopped fresh chives*
*2 tablespoons chopped flat-leaf parsley*
*2 tablespoons heavy cream*
*2 tablespoons Curry Butter (see Appendices)*

METHOD Place the kuri squash juice in a medium saucepan and simmer for 45 minutes, or until reduced to 4 cups of juice. Pass through a fine-mesh sieve, and return to the saucepan. Whisk in 2 tablespoons of the butter and season to taste with salt and pepper.

Cut the squash in half and remove the seeds. Season the inside with the olive oil, salt, and pepper. Place cut side down on a sheet pan with ¼ inch water and bake at 375 degrees for 45 minutes, or until tender. Scoop out the pulp from the squash and coarsely chop. Place the pulp in a small bowl with 1 tablespoon of butter, season to taste with salt and pepper, and set aside.

To make the spätzle, combine the egg and milk in a small bowl and whisk until fully incorporated. Stir in the flour, season with salt and pepper, and fold in the chives and parsley. Place the spätzle batter in a small funnel or pastry bag. Drop ¼ teaspoon-size spoonfuls into boiling salted water and cook for 1 minute. Transfer the dumplings to a sauté pan with the remaining 2 tablespoons of butter. Over medium heat, lightly brown the spätzle and season to taste with salt and pepper. Heat the heavy cream in a small saucepan and slowly whisk in the Curry Butter.

ASSEMBLY Place a quenelle of the kuri squash in the center of each bowl, spoon in some of the broth, and arrange the spätzle around the edge of the bowl. Drizzle the Curry Butter mixture in the broth and top with freshly ground black pepper.

## Wine Notes

These flavors are naturally sweet and enriched further by the butter and curry high tones. Spätzle provides a textural foil with a delicate herbal balance to the squash's sweetness. Wines with some residual sugar will meet the sweet flavors well while enhancing the spice effects. *Vendange tardive* wines from Alsace are the most attractive, though Gewürztraminer takes the spice component too far; Pinot Gris is a more satisfying varietal choice. One of the most incredible wines we know for this dish is the *Clos Windsbuhl* Pinot Gris by Zind Humbrecht; the 1991 is sensationally rich and long at the finish. On a lighter note, Demi-Sec Champagne will be effective with the broth while delivering slight sweetness; try Moët et Chandon.

# Cold Kashi Salad with Dried Cranberries, Celery, White Pumpkin, Pumpkin Seeds, and Pumpkin Seed Oil

*I have always loved grain salads. Plus, it is easy to make a large quantity and keep it in the refrigerator for a couple of days for quick snacks. The other great advantage of grain salads is that they can be easily heated and enjoyed warm separately or used as an accompaniment. Grain salads are also quite versatile because their ingredients are so interchangeable.*

**Serves 4**

*1 small white pumpkin*
*1½ tablespoons olive oil*
*Salt and pepper*
*2½ cups cooked and cooled kashi*
*⅓ cup dried cranberries*
*⅓ cup peeled and thinly sliced celery*
*½ cup thinly sliced red onion*
*2 tablespoons pumpkin seed oil*

METHOD Cut the pumpkin in half and place the seeds in a small bowl. Season with 2 teaspoons olive oil, salt, and pepper. Place on a sheet pan cut side down with ¼ inch of water. Bake at 375 degrees for 45 minutes, or until tender. Let cool and remove the skin. Cut the pumpkin into large dice and set aside (you should have about 1½ cups). Remove and discard the pulp strands from the seeds and toss with the remaining olive oil. Spread the seeds on a sheet pan and bake at 300 degrees for 30 minutes, or until golden brown and crisp.

Place the kashi, cranberries, celery, red onion, diced pumpkin, and pumpkin seed oil in a medium bowl. Toss together and season to taste with salt and pepper. Fold in the pumpkin seeds and serve immediately.

ASSEMBLY Place a mound of the kashi salad in the center of each plate and top with freshly ground black pepper.

**Wine Notes**

The dried cranberries add a chewy dimension to the nutlike grain mixture here, while celery adds crunch and bridges the flavors. And the pumpkin seed oil adds an intense nutty flavor itself. Many wines will also connect these flavors, especially dry Rosés from the south of France and some Italian white wines, like Fiano di Avellino. Even slightly oaky French Chardonnays will be useful; we caution, however, against higher-acid varieties like Riesling and cool-climate Sauvignon Blanc. Rhônes are a touch hefty and aromatic varieties are a bit awkward.

# Roasted Root Vegetable Ragout with Braised Red Cabbage and Chestnut Purée

*The sweetness of a medley of root vegetables is hard to top when the weather gets cold.*
*Accented by a little braised purple cabbage and wisps of red onion, the combination*
*becomes truly delectable. The* coup de grace *is the addition of the resplendent chestnuts, which*
*provides a fascinating texture as well as a mature, controlled sweetness.*

**Serves 4**

*2 large carrots*

*2 large parsnips*

*1 small red onion*

*1 celery root*

*1 turnip*

*1 small rutabaga*

*5 tablespoons butter*

*2 cups red cabbage, coarsely chopped*

*1 cup red wine*

*1 tablespoon rice vinegar*

*2 tablespoons sugar*

*Salt and pepper*

*1/2 cup coarsely chopped roasted chestnuts*

*3/4 cup water*

*2 tablespoons chopped chervil*

METHOD Place the carrots, parsnips, red onion, celery root, turnip, and rutabaga on a sheet pan and roast at 400 degrees for 2 to 3½ hours, or until the vegetables are tender (the carrots and parsnips will take less time than the larger vegetables). Once cool, remove the dark outer layer of the peel from the vegetables. Cut the vegetables into oblique-shape wedges. Place 2 tablespoons of the butter and the cabbage in a large sauté pan. Cook over medium-high heat for 5 minutes, then add the red wine, rice vinegar, and sugar. Continue to cook for 10 to 12 minutes, or until the cabbage is tender. Season to taste with salt and pepper. Drain the cooking juice from the cabbage, place the liquid in a small saucepan, and whisk in 1 tablespoon of the butter.

Place 6 tablespoons of the chestnuts in a small saucepan with the water and bring to a simmer. Place in a blender and purée until smooth. Return to the saucepan, season to taste with salt and pepper, and keep warm. Place the oblique-cut vegetables in a large sauté pan with the remaining 2 tablespoons butter and warm over medium-high heat. Season to taste with salt and pepper and toss with the chopped chervil.

ASSEMBLY Layer some of the roasted vegetables and purple cabbage in the center of each plate. Spoon the chestnut purée and cabbage cooking liquid around the vegetables. Arrange some of the chestnut pieces around the plate. Top with freshly ground black pepper.

**Wine Notes**

Clean, yet somewhat earthy flavors are needed to balance the onion's pungency and the sweetness of the root vegetables. Chestnuts add a creamy nuttiness, and the red cabbage adds sweetness. The Mâcon-Pierreclos by Guffens-Heynen is a clean Chardonnay with a light touch of oak, and it marries well with all of these elements, especially with the chestnuts. Manzanilla Sherry accompanies the nutty flavors perfectly, but seems a touch light in weight and high in alcohol. Rhône whites are less successful than Burgundies and other Chardonnays; Hermitage and Châteauneuf-du-Pape are hard and also too high in alcohol.

# Crispy Polenta with Portobello Mushrooms, Wilted Greens, and Pomegranate-Balsamic Vinaigrette

*The portobello mushrooms in this preparation are meatlike in their earthy richness.*
*The pomegranate element adds the perfect edge of refreshing sweetness.*
*The effect is even more full-flavored than it might otherwise be because of the lightly wilted tatsoi,*
*which nicely cuts into the two elements and magnificently highlights their contrasting flavors.*
*The Veal Stock Reduction enriches the entire dish and gives it a beautiful richness.*

**Serves 4**

*2 cups hot cooked polenta*

*4 tablespoons butter*

*Salt and pepper*

*2 pomegranates*

*2 teaspoons 12-year-old balsamic vinegar*

*3 tablespoons olive oil*

*2 portobello mushrooms, roasted*

*2 cups mizuna*

*2 cups tatsoi*

*1 tablespoon water*

*¼ cup Veal Stock Reduction*
*(see Appendices)*

METHOD  Mix the soft, just cooked polenta with 2 tablespoons of the butter and season to taste with salt and pepper. Spread the mixture out on a flat surface into a layer about ½ inch thick, cover with plastic wrap, and refrigerate for 2 hours.

Cut open the pomegranates and carefully remove all of the seeds. Reserve ¼ cup of the seeds. Place the remaining seeds in a blender, purée for 15 seconds, then pass through a fine-mesh sieve. Place the pomegranate juice in a small saucepan and simmer for 15 to 20 minutes, or until the juice is reduced by half and coats the back of a spoon. Place 1½ tablespoons of the pomegranate reduction in a small bowl with the balsamic vinegar. Slowly whisk in the olive oil, season to taste with salt and pepper, and fold in the reserved pomegranate seeds.

Using a round 2½-inch cutter, cut the cooled polenta into 4 discs. Place the discs in a nonstick sauté pan with 2 teaspoons of the butter. Cook over medium-high heat for 3 minutes on each side, or until golden brown and crisp. Remove to paper towels and keep warm.

Cut the portobello mushrooms into ¼-inch-thick pieces and place in a sauté pan with 1 teaspoon of the butter. Cook over medium heat for 3 minutes, or until hot. Season to taste with salt and pepper. Quickly wilt the greens with the remaining 1 tablespoon of butter and a tablespoon of water in a hot sauté pan and season to taste with salt and pepper. Place the Veal Stock Reduction in a small saucepan and warm over medium heat.

ASSEMBLY  Place some of the wilted greens in the center of each plate. Lay one of the polenta discs on the greens and top with the remaining wilted greens. Arrange the portobello mushrooms on top of the greens. Lightly spoon some of the pomegranate vinaigrette and pomegranate seeds over the mushrooms and around the plate. Spoon the Veal Stock Reduction over the mushrooms and around the plate. Top with freshly ground black pepper.

## Wine Notes

The mushroom flavors combine with the meat juices to make red wines useful here, even a wine as powerful as a Côte-Rotie or Saint Joseph from a lighter vintage. These wines have a great peppery perfume without the tannin one finds in Hermitage or southern Rhône appellations like Gigondas or Châteauneuf-du-Pape. Lighter Burgundy works in a similar fashion; any number of 1992 red Burgundies will be appropriate despite a slight clash with the pomegranate.

# Arun's Phad Thai
# with Wood Ear Mushrooms

*Arun Sampanthavivat, one of my great culinary friends in Chicago, is one of the*
*most creative and poetic individuals I know. His style comes across*
*the moment you enter his elegant restaurant, Arun's, on Chicago's north side.*
*He graciously gave me his recipe for Phad Thai, one of my favorite dishes.*
*Aside from the addition of wood ear mushrooms, I have followed his masterpiece to the letter.*

## Serves 4

*4 teaspoons minced garlic*

*1/2 cup peeled and small-diced turnip*

*2 tablespoons grapeseed oil*

*1 cup coarsely chopped fresh wood ear mushrooms*

*1 small dried red chile pepper, finely chopped*

*1 cup firm tofu, cut in medium dice*

*1/4 cup Thai fish sauce*

*2 teaspoons rice vinegar*

*3 tablespoons sugar*

*4 teaspoons paprika*

*4 tablespoons tamarind juice*

*4 cups medium-width rice noodles, soaked in cold water for 30 minutes, or until slightly limp, and drained*

*1 1/2 cups water*

*1/2 cup ground peanuts, toasted*

*2 cups mung bean sprouts*

*1 cup garlic chives, cut into 1/2-inch pieces on the bias*

*Juice of 1 lime*

*Salt and pepper*

*1 lime, peeled and cut into small sections*

*1/2 cup peanuts, toasted and halved*

METHOD  In a wok or large sauté pan, stir-fry the garlic, turnips, and grapeseed oil. Add the mushrooms, chile pepper, and tofu and cook, stirring, for 2 minutes. In a small bowl, combine the Thai fish sauce, vinegar, sugar, paprika, and tamarind juice. Add the Thai fish sauce mixture, rice noodles, and water to the wok. Continue to stir-fry and gently toss until most of the water is absorbed. Stir in the ground peanuts, bean sprouts, garlic chives, and lime juice, and season to taste with salt and pepper.

ASSEMBLY  Place a mound of Phad Thai in the center of each plate. Arrange some of the lime sections and peanuts over the Phad Thai.

## Wine Notes

Liberal use of heat in the dish requires a low-alcohol wine, or even better, a grain-based beverage. Momokawa Sake is low-acid, food-friendly, and dry and refreshing enough with the spicy presence, even though its alcohol level (15 percent) is high. Crisp, hoppy beers are the best matches: favorites include the great Pilsner Urquell and the rounder, maltier Anchor Steam beer. We recommend staying away from light beers and Weiss styles. Some intensely aromatic wines have appeal too: Graacher Himmelreich Kabinett by J. J. Prüm is a crisp match with plenty of spritz, and Condrieu by Cuilleron thrills on its own and adds a floral component; however, it possesses a texturally awkward oiliness that seems too rich for the subtle flavors of the sauce and the mushrooms.

# Warm Apple Tart with Date Ice Cream and Red Wine—Caramel Sauce

*This is a dramatic variation on a classic apple tart. The Red Wine—Caramel Sauce, flecked with roasted pecans, is a lot more complex than standard caramel sauce and is not as sweet. The date ice cream is so satisfying it could be eaten by itself, but with the succulent apples and the elegant caramel sauce you have the makings of a simple yet highly sophisticated dessert.*

**Serves 4**

*1 cup Burgundy*

*1½ cups sugar*

*4 tablespoons butter*

*1 vanilla bean, split lengthwise with the pulp scraped out and reserved*

*3 Granny Smith apples, peeled and cut into 20 thick wedges*

*Pâté Brisée (see Appendices)*

*5 tablespoons chopped pecans*

*Date Ice Cream (recipe follows)*

METHOD Place the Burgundy in a small saucepan and simmer for 20 minutes, or until reduced to ¼ cup. Place the sugar in a medium saucepan. Gently melt the sugar over medium-low heat until golden brown. Add the butter and vanilla pulp and continue to cook for 2 minutes. Add the apple wedges and cook for 5 to 7 minutes, or until the apples are half cooked. Remove the apples from the caramel and reserve both separately.

Roll out the Pâté Brisée ⅛ inch thick and line four 2¾ by ½-inch ring or tart molds (other molds of a similar size will also work). Place the molds on a parchment-lined sheet pan. Line the bottom of each mold with ½ teaspoon of the chopped pecans. Place 4 to 5 apple wedges in each tart and brush with some of the caramel sauce.

Add the remaining caramel sauce to the red wine reduction and whisk until smooth. Fold in the remaining pecans and keep warm.

Place the tarts in the oven at 350 degrees for 20 to 30 minutes, or until golden brown. Remove from the molds and use immediately.

ASSEMBLY Place an apple tart in the center of each plate. Spoon the Red Wine—Caramel Sauce around the tart and place a scoop of the Date Ice Cream at the top of the center of the plate.

## Date Ice Cream

Yield: 1 quart

*14 ounces dried dates, pitted and chopped*

*Pulp of 1 vanilla bean*

*1½ cups heavy cream*

*¾ cup half-and-half*

*¾ cup milk*

*6 egg yolks*

METHOD Place the dates, vanilla bean pulp, heavy cream, half-and-half, and milk in a medium saucepan. Bring to a simmer over medium heat. Place the yolks in a medium bowl and whisk until smooth. Slowly pour the cream mixture into the yolks while continually whisking.

Place in a blender and purée until smooth. Return to the saucepan and cook for 3 minutes, stirring constantly. Pass through a fine-mesh sieve, then cool. Freeze in an ice cream machine, and keep frozen until ready to use.

## Wine Notes

Sweet, unctuous late-harvest Riesling seems to dovetail with the apple and date combination, but only older styles of Beerenauslese or Trockenbeerenauslese will have the desired balance and toned-down acidity. We also find that sweet Tokaji Aszu is practical at the 5 or 6 puttonyos level, as it is texturally rich enough and sweet enough for the caramel sauce. The *Birsalma's* single-vineyard Tokaji is an invigorating, sumptuous match.

*Let the sky rain potatoes.* WILLIAM SHAKESPEARE

**December** air is undeniably sharp, but I am so filled with holiday cheer and an insatiable appetite that I hardly notice. Many memorable meals with friends and family are to be enjoyed. ❧  I love yams and root vegetables and any type of grain in December. I especially love barley served with a broth. Puréed potato soup is also most satisfying with perhaps the added indulgence of black truffles. Hokkaido squash is splendid with its elegant sweetness and works wonderfully with all exotic spices. Sunchokes and water chestnuts can add a hint of sweetness to any soup or broth. I particularly desire ultrasimple foods, such as whole roasted cauliflower or broccoli. With a little drizzle of olive oil or butter, or when served in a broth, these two everyday foodstuffs become truly profound. December is the one month I simply don't worry about what I eat, as achieving gustatory satisfaction is my sole goal. I'll worry about the consequences on January 1.

# Baby Turnip and Beet Ragout with Scallion Sauce and Beet Oil

~~~~~~~~~~~~~~~~~~~~~~~~~~~~~~~~~~~~~~~~~~~~~~~~~~~~~~~~~~~

*This ragout is like a little taste of summer in the winter. The flavors of the turnips and beets are sweet and delicate, but they are also robust. The braised scallions and scallion sauce add an incredible vibrance and almost a poetic sharpness that is not too sharp. The beet nicely reinforces the elegant sweetness of the root vegetables and the concentrated vegetable stock ties all of the flavors together.*

**Serves 4**

*16 Parisian carrots, peeled*
*16 kabu (Japanese baby turnips), peeled*
*1 teaspoon grapeseed oil*
*Salt and pepper*
*16 baby red beets*
*16 baby yellow beets*
*16 candystripe beets*
*3 sprigs rosemary*
*3 bunches scallions*
*2 cups Vegetable Stock (see Appendices)*
*¼ cup Beet Oil (recipe follows)*
*½ cup Scallion Sauce (recipe follows)*

METHOD In a medium bowl, toss the carrots and kabu with the grapeseed oil and season with salt and pepper. Place on a sheet pan and roast at 350 degrees for about 15 minutes, or until golden brown. Cook each type of baby beet separately in a small saucepan with 1 sprig of the rosemary and enough water to cover. Simmer 10 to 15 minutes, or until the skin can be easily removed. Peel the beets and set them aside in separate bowls (the colors bleed). Cut the tip of the root end off the scallions, and cut them in half, dividing the white and the green portions (the green ends are for the scallion sauce). Slowly braise the white ends of the scallions in the Vegetable Stock for 5 to 7 minutes, or until limp. Remove from the liquid and season to taste with salt and pepper.

ASSEMBLY Arrange 4 each of the hot cooked beets, carrots, and turnips on each plate along with the scallions. Drizzle the Beet Oil and Scallion Sauce around the vegetables.

## Beet Oil

Yield: about ⅓ cup

*6 large red beets*
*2 tablespoons grapeseed oil*

METHOD Peel and juice the beets. Simmer the beet juice in a small saucepan for 30 to 40 minutes, or until it is reduced by three-quarters and coats the back of a spoon. Strain through a fine-mesh sieve. Blend the beet reduction with the grapeseed oil and set aside.

## Scallion Sauce

Yield: about ½ cup

*3 bunches scallion greens (reserved from ragout)*
*2 tablespoons olive oil*
*2 teaspoons grapeseed oil*
*¼ cup water (approximately)*
*Salt and pepper*

METHOD Blanch the scallion greens in boiling salted water. Shock in ice water and drain. Coarsely chop the greens and place in a blender. With the blender on low, slowly add the olive oil and grapeseed oil and just enough water for the liquid to purée smoothly. Strain through a fine-mesh sieve and season to taste with salt and pepper. If it is too thick, adjust by adding a little water.

### Wine Notes

With this dish, individual wine and vegetable connections are more easily made than a total match. The various beets, with their earthy sweetness, flower with the flavor of a Zind Humbrecht Gewürztraminer. The baby turnip, however, shines with the drier Marsanne of August Clape's Côtes du Rhône Blanc. The Parisian carrot merges well with another Alsatian wine, the Pinot Gris *Reserve Personelle* of Kuentz-Bas. All together, these roots work best with Hermitage Blanc, a style that offers heady aromas and firm structure.

# Roasted Matsutake and Cauliflower Mushrooms with Barley, Water Chestnuts, Sunchokes, and Mushroom Broth

*This dish is simple, but the flavors are quite profound.*
*The matsutake mushrooms have a complex flavor and the cauliflower mushrooms almost*
*melt like butter. The barley is perfectly toothsome, giving a meatlike effect.*
*The sunchokes and water chestnuts add the perfect textural foil, and the crown—the elegance—*
*comes from the mushroom broth, which can be made to any degree of strength.*

**Serves 4**

*1 1/2 pounds button mushrooms, cleaned*

*2 cups matsutake mushrooms, cleaned*

*2 cups cauliflower mushrooms, cleaned*

*7 teaspoons olive oil*

*Salt and pepper*

*3 sprigs rosemary*

*2 cloves garlic*

*8 fresh water chestnuts*

*3/4 cup raw barley*

*2 1/4 cups water or Chicken Stock
(see Appendices)*

*1 sunchoke (Jerusalem artichoke)*

*2 cups loosely packed baby red Swiss chard*

METHOD Place the button mushrooms in a large stockpot and cover with water. Simmer for 2 1/2 to 3 hours, or until reduced by three-quarters. Strain, discard button mushrooms, and set aside broth. Place the matsutake and cauliflower mushrooms in separate ovenproof pans, drizzle 2 teaspoons of the olive oil over each type of mushroom, and season with salt and pepper. Place a sprig of rosemary and a whole clove of garlic in each pan, cover with aluminum foil and roast at 350 degrees for about 45 minutes, or until just done.

Cover the water chestnuts with water, bring to a boil, and then reduce heat to simmer for 10 minutes, or until tender. Peel the water chestnuts and cut into 8 wedges. Place the raw barley on a sheet pan and roast in the oven at 350 degrees for 10 to 12 minutes, or until it starts to turn golden brown. Place the barley and 2 1/4 cups water in a 2-quart saucepan with the remaining sprig of rosemary. Simmer, stirring occasionally, for 40 to 50 minutes, or until the barley is thoroughly cooked (it will have tripled in volume). Peel and julienne the sunchoke. In a small sauté pan, lightly caramelize the sunchoke in 2 teaspoons of olive oil for 2 to 3 minutes, until golden brown. In a medium sauté pan, bring 2 tablespoons of water and the remaining tablespoon of olive oil to a simmer. Add the Swiss chard and turn off the heat. Toss gently until slightly wilted, remove from the pan, season with salt and pepper, and set aside.

ASSEMBLY Place some cooked barley in each bowl. Sprinkle the water chestnuts and sunchokes around the barley and arrange the mushrooms on top. Place the red Swiss chard around the edge of the bowl and ladle in some mushroom broth.

## Wine Notes

This rich and satisfying dish allows the sweet water chestnut flavor to peek through the warm, savory flavors of mushroom and barley. Here is an occasion for a rich Chardonnay. The toastiness of new oak in the Peter Michael *Cuvée Indigene*, fermented with natural yeasts, complements all of these elements. This preparation could lean more toward red wines with a richer mushroom broth and liberal use of black pepper. With these adjustments, a delicate Burgundy from the Côte de Nuits is very pleasurable.

# Roasted Hokkaido, Buttercup, Red Kuri, and De Lacota Squashes with Star Anise–Infused Vegetable Broth

*I have a sweet tooth, and I do not mean just for dessert. I have always been drawn to sweet foods. That's why I love a dish like this—different kinds of squash, roasted, sweet, and simple in their essences. The star anise–infused vegetable broth transforms this preparation into something profound.*

**Serves 4**

*1 hokkaido squash*
*1 buttercup squash*
*1 red kuri squash*
*1 de lacota squash*
*¼ cup olive oil*
*Salt and pepper*
*6 cups Roasted Vegetable Stock (see Appendices)*
*2 star anise*

METHOD Cut each squash into wedges, remove the seeds, toss with olive oil, and season with salt and pepper. Place on a sheet pan and roast at 350 degrees for 15 to 20 minutes. Turn the squash and continue cooking for 15 to 20 minutes, or until thoroughly cooked. Remove and season to taste with salt and pepper. In a saucepan, simmer and slowly reduce the Roasted Vegetable Stock with the star anise for 45 minutes, or until reduced by half.

ASSEMBLY Arrange the squash in each bowl. Ladle the Roasted Vegetable Stock into each bowl. Garnish with star anise if desired.

**Wine Notes**

These sweet roasted squashes need a wine with a suggestion of sweetness, yet with plenty of richness and length. Condrieu provides this, and succeeds in richer styles, like that of Guigal or Vernay. A tasting of Alsatian Gewürztraminer (the Zind Humbrecht *Heimbourg*) made a fantastic aromatic connection with the star anise, but seemed too sweet at the finish. A leaner Gewürztraminer, such as Ostertag's, could be delightful.

# White Rose Potato Soup with Black Truffles and Thyme

*Although this soup is creamy, it is made without cream, which means
you can really taste the purity and elegant saltiness of the white rose potatoes.
Black truffles burst with flavor against this pure backdrop, and
the radishes and turnips add a refined salient edge.*

**Serves 4**

23 (2-inch) white rose potatoes

1 cup milk

3 shallots, diced

2 cloves garlic, minced

1 teaspoon grapeseed oil

5 cups Blond Vegetable Stock
(see Appendices)

Salt and pepper

1 bleeding heart radish, peeled and julienned

1 red satin radish, julienned

1 teaspoon freshly squeezed lemon juice

1 black truffle

3 sprigs thyme, leaves removed

1 tablespoon Chive Oil (recipe follows)

METHOD Cut 15 of the potatoes into wedges and place in a large pot. Add the milk and cover with water. Bring to a simmer and cook until the potatoes are falling apart. In a small sauté pan, sweat the shallots and garlic in the grapeseed oil and set aside. Strain the potatoes and place in a food processor or blender with the shallot-garlic mixture. With the blender on low, slowly add the Blond Vegetable Stock and purée until smooth. Strain through a fine-mesh sieve. Place the mixture in a medium saucepan and cook over very low heat until a subtle sweetness comes through. Season with salt and pepper and set aside. Cut the remaining 8 potatoes into 30 slices, approximately 1/8 inch thick. Trim each slice into a round disc about the size of a half-dollar. Place the potato discs into a pot and cover with salted water. Bring to a slow simmer, but do not boil, for about 10 to 12 minutes, or until tender. In a medium bowl, toss the bleeding heart radish and the red satin radish with the lemon juice. Slice the black truffle paper-thin, then take one-quarter of the sliced truffles, julienne, and toss with the radish mixture.

ASSEMBLY In each bowl, layer the potato discs with the truffle slices to make 6 layers of potatoes and truffles. Top with the radish mixture. Ladle the soup into the bowl and sprinkle with the thyme leaves and Chive Oil.

## Chive Oil

Yield: 1 cup

2 cups chives

1 1/3 cups grapeseed oil

2/3 cup olive oil

METHOD Blanch the chives in boiling salted water for 7 seconds, shock in ice water, and drain. Coarsely chop the chives and squeeze out any excess liquid. Place in a blender with the oil and purée until bright green. Pour into a container, cover, and refrigerate for 1 day. Strain through cheesecloth and refrigerate for 1 more day, and then decant.

## Wine Notes

The aromatic enticement of this lovely preparation invites several aromatic wine choices. Riesling is wonderful with the thyme yet is not enough for the truffle influence. Northern Rhône selections, based on the Marsanne grape, provide richness and complexity to match the truffle and thyme. Hermitage Blanc by Grippat seems an appropriate wine. Texturally, the wine's fuller flavor stands up to the silky soup.

# Celery Root Ravioli with Celery and Mushroom Filling and Red Wine Reduction

*This is my version of a wonderful dish I once had at Marc Veyrat's fantastic restaurant in Annecy, France.*
*Thin sheets of celery root are used in lieu of pasta to create an interesting, playful effect.*
*Here I have devised a filling of portobello mushrooms and celery leaves, but almost anything works well*
*with celery root. The full-flavored red wine sauce instantly weaves all the elements together.*

**Serves 4**

*½ cup diced carrot*

*½ cup diced celery*

*½ cup diced Spanish onion*

*6 teaspoons olive oil*

*2 large celery roots, peeled*

*3 large portobello mushrooms*

*Salt and pepper*

*1 clove garlic*

*1 sprig rosemary*

*1 stalk celery, diced*

*1 tablespoon diced shallot*

*2 tablespoons chopped parsley, chives,*
*or other fresh herbs*

*2 cups flat-leaf parsley leaves*

*1 cup Red Wine Reduction (see Appendices)*

METHOD In a medium saucepan, caramelize the carrots, celery, and onion in 2 teaspoons of the olive oil. Add the celery root, cover three-quarters of the way with water, and cover the pan. Slowly braise for 45 to 60 minutes, or until tender. Remove the celery root from the braising liquid and cool completely. Reserve the braising liquid. Trim the celery root to square off and slice paper-thin. Clean the portobello mushrooms by removing the stems and the dark brown underside. Cut into quarters, season with salt and pepper, and drizzle with 2 teaspoons of the olive oil. Place in an ovenproof pan with the garlic and rosemary and cover with aluminum foil. Bake at 350 degrees for 30 to 40 minutes, or until tender.

In a medium sauté pan, sauté the diced celery and shallot in 1 teaspoon of the olive oil. Dice the roasted mushrooms and toss with the celery mixture and herbs. In a sauté pan, wilt the parsley in 1 teaspoon of the olive oil and 1 tablespoon of the braising liquid. Place the celery root slices on a sheet pan with a dash of the braising liquid, season with salt and pepper, and bake at 350 degrees for 3 to 4 minutes to reheat.

ASSEMBLY Lay 1 slice of the celery root on a plate and top with the mushroom and celery mixture. Place a piece of the parsley on top and cover with another piece of the celery root. Press the edges of the celery root together and place small pinches of braised parsley at each corner. Drizzle the Red Wine Reduction around the edges of each plate.

**Wine Notes**

White Rhônes are the most attractive option here, yet a Condrieu can overpower with too much alcohol. Hermitage Blanc seems to carry the complex rooty flavors well. One must be careful with the flat-leaf parsley, which can overtake the palate in spite of any wine flavors. Another useful wine is the Pinot Auxerrois *H* by JosMeyer, whose Alsatian *terroir* flavors form a fine emphasis to the mushroom filling and allow the delicate celery flavor to shine.

# Roasted Whole Cauliflower with Broccoli Juice

*This simple preparation combines two of the most common and underappreciated vegetables:
cauliflower and broccoli. I especially like roasting a head of cauliflower to really
concentrate the flavor and bring out the wonderful sweetness. The broccoli appears in two forms,
puréed and as a juice, which makes for fascinating textural contrasts.*

### Serves 4

*1 small head of cauliflower*

*1 teaspoon grapeseed oil*

*Salt and pepper*

*1 head of broccoli*

*1 tablespoon water*

*1 tablespoon butter*

*1 tablespoon olive oil*

METHOD Trim the stem and remove the leaves from the cauliflower. Lightly rub with grapeseed oil and season with salt and pepper. Place on a sheet pan with ½ inch of water and roast at 350 degrees for 1½ hours, until tender and brown on the edges (keep ½ inch of water in the pan at all times).

Juice the broccoli stems and half of the broccoli florets. Blanch the remaining florets in boiling salted water. Place blanched florets in a blender with 1 tablespoon of water and purée until smooth. Season to taste with salt and pepper and keep warm.

In a saucepan, heat the broccoli juice, whisking in the butter and olive oil just as it starts to simmer. Remove from heat, and season to taste with salt and pepper. Serve immediately.

ASSEMBLY Slice the cauliflower vertically into 4 pieces, retaining its natural shape. Place 1 slice in each bowl. Place a quenelle of the broccoli purée on top of the cauliflower. Ladle the broccoli sauce around the cauliflower.

### Wine Notes

The roasted, nutty quality of the cauliflower is balanced by the sweet, nearly herbal broccoli purée. A wine of fairly high acidity will match the clean, high-acid broccoli flavor while complementing the slight richness imparted by the butter and oil. Most successful are styles of Halbtrocken Riesling from the Rheingau (a great match with the broccoli juice) and Albarino from western Spain, whose slight earthiness underscores both crucifer flavors.

# Yam and Pistachio Custard Tart with Turmeric Anglaise Sauce

*Pistachios and yams bring to mind pastries I've had in Jerusalem that feature carrots and pistachios. The especially flaky pastry, suggestive of filo, also recalls the Middle East. With the addition of candied turmeric, you'll delight in this exotically flavored dessert.*

**Serves 4 to 6**

*1 (12-ounce) yam, peeled*

*2 eggs*

*²/₃ cup plus 2 tablespoons heavy cream*

*1¹/₃ cups sugar*

*¹/₈ teaspoon ground cinnamon*

*¹/₈ teaspoon ground nutmeg*

*¹/₈ teaspoon ground allspice*

*1 cup pistachios, roasted*

*2 tablespoons julienned fresh turmeric*

*Pâté Brisée (see Appendices)*

*¹/₂ cup Anglaise Sauce (see Appendices)*

METHOD  Place the yam on a sheet pan and roast in the oven at 350 degrees for 1 hour, or until very soft. Purée the yam in a food processor until smooth. (You should have about 1 cup of purée.) In a medium bowl, whisk together the eggs, ²/₃ cup of the heavy cream, and ¹/₃ cup of the sugar. Whisk the yam purée into the cream mixture until smooth. Season with the cinnamon, nutmeg, and allspice and refrigerate until needed.

Place three-quarters of the roasted pistachios and the remaining 2 tablespoons heavy cream in a blender and purée. Place the julienned turmeric in a small saucepan with ¹/₂ cup of the sugar, cover with water, and bring to a simmer. Drain, and repeat with fresh water and the remaining ¹/₂ cup sugar. Simmer for about 15 minutes, or until tender. Strain the turmeric and set aside. Return the cooking liquid to the heat and simmer for about 15 minutes, or until it coats the back of a spoon.

On a floured work surface roll the Pâté Brisée ¹/₈ inch thick. Place 4 ring molds (3-inches-wide by ¹/₂-inch-high ring molds are best, but similar sizes will also work) on a parchment-lined sheet pan and line the ring molds with the dough. Spread a thin coat of the pistachio purée in the bottom of the dough-filled mold. Fill the molds with the custard and sprinkle with the remaining chopped pistachios. Place the sheet pan in the oven and bake at 375 degrees for about 30 minutes, or until the tart puffs and is slightly firm to the touch. Remove from the oven and serve warm.

ASSEMBLY  Place a tart in the center of each plate and drizzle the Anglaise Sauce and turmeric syrup around it. At three points, place small mounds of the candied turmeric.

**Wine Notes**

This dessert is unabashedly sweet, demanding a rather sweet dessert wine. Classic Sauternes from a great vintage provide the best flavor. Château Rieussec 1983 is a good example. The honeyed flavors of Botrytized Sauternes can match the exotic turmeric flavor, and the slightly caramelized flavors of maturity in this type of wine help carry the nutty pistachio influence.

# APPENDICES

Juices and Syrups

Oils

Reductions and Stocks

Other Basics

Cooking Terms, Equipment, Ingredients
and Techniques

Sources

## Juices and Syrups

### Mint Syrup

Yield: about 1 cup

*2 cups fresh mint leaves*
*1 cup sugar*
*1/2 cup water*

METHOD  Blanch the mint in boiling salted water and shock in ice water. Strain, squeeze out the excess water, and coarsely chop the mint. In a small saucepan, combine the sugar and water and simmer for 15 minutes, or until it reaches a thick syrupy consistency. Remove from heat and cool completely. Place the mint and the sugar syrup in a blender and purée on medium for 3 to 5 minutes, or until smooth. Place in a container and store in the refrigerator overnight. Strain through a fine-mesh sieve, then refrigerate for 1 more day before decanting.

### Mushroom Juice

Yield: about 1/2 cup

*1 cup wild mushrooms (such as portobello, shiitake, cremini), cleaned*
*1/4 cup peeled and chopped Spanish onion*
*1 sprig thyme*
*1 tablespoon olive oil*
*1/2 cup water*
*Salt and pepper*

METHOD  Place the mushrooms in an oven-proof pan with the onion, thyme, olive oil, and water. Season with salt and pepper. Cover and bake in the oven at 375 degrees for 30 minutes, or until the mushrooms are tender. Remove from the oven and strain the cooking liquid through a fine-mesh sieve. This will be the mushroom juice. (Use the roasted mushrooms in another dish; they will keep nicely in the refrigerator for a couple of days.)

### Parsley Juice

Yield: 3/4 cup

*1 bunch flat-leaf parsley*
*1/4 cup grapeseed oil*
*1/4 cup ice water*
*Salt and pepper*

METHOD  In a very hot pan, sauté the parsley for a few seconds in 1 tablespoon of the grapeseed oil. Immediately remove from the pan and place in the refrigerator. Coarsely chop the cooled parsley and place in a blender with the ice water and remaining 3 tablespoons of grapeseed oil.

Blend thoroughly and strain through a fine-mesh sieve. Season to taste with salt and pepper and store in the refrigerator until needed.

### Pickling Juice

Yield: 2 cups

*1 cup water*
*1/2 cup rice vinegar*
*1/3 cup plus 2 tablespoons sugar*
*2 tablespoons kosher salt*
*1 whole clove*
*1 teaspoon mustard seed*
*1 teaspoon black peppercorns*
*1 teaspoon chopped gingerroot*
*1/2 jalapeño, seeded and chopped*

METHOD  Combine all of the ingredients in a small saucepan and bring to a simmer, allowing the salt and sugar to dissolve. Cool and use as needed.

### Red Bell Pepper Juice

Yield: about 1/3 cup

*3 red bell peppers, seeded*

METHOD  Juice the peppers and place in a medium saucepan. Over medium heat, reduce the liquid for 20 minutes, or until it has a light syrup-like consistency. Strain through a fine-mesh sieve and store in the refrigerator until needed.

### Simple Syrup

Yield: 6 cups

*3 cups sugar*
*3 cups water*

METHOD  Combine the sugar and water in a medium saucepan. Bring to a boil, stirring until all the sugar is dissolved. Remove from heat and cool. The syrup will keep indefinitely in the refrigerator.

## Oils

### Basil Oil

Yield: 1 1/2 cups

*3 cups basil*
*1 cup grapeseed oil*
*1 cup olive oil*

METHOD  Blanch the basil in boiling salted water for 15 seconds. Immediately shock in ice water and drain. Coarsely chop the basil and squeeze out the excess water. Place in a blender with the oil and purée for 3 to 4 minutes, or until bright green. Pour into a container, cover, and refrigerate for 1 day. Strain through cheesecloth, refrigerate for 1 more day, and then decant.

### Coriander Oil

Yield: 1/2 cup

*1 cup coriander*
*1/4 cup grapeseed oil*
*1/4 cup olive oil*

METHOD  Blanch the coriander in boiling salted water for 15 seconds. Immediately shock in ice water and drain. Coarsely chop the coriander and squeeze out the excess water. Place into a blender with the two oils. Purée for 3 to 4 minutes, or until bright green. Pour into a container, cover, and refrigerate for 1 day. Strain through cheesecloth, refrigerate for 1 more day, and then decant.

### Dill Oil

Yield: 1 cup

*2 cups dill*
*1 1/2 cups grapeseed oil*
*1/2 cup olive oil*

METHOD  Blanch the dill in boiling salted water for 15 seconds. Immediately shock in ice water and drain. Coarsely chop the dill and squeeze out the excess water. Place in a blender with the oil, and purée for 3 or 4 minutes, or until bright green. Pour into a container, cover, and refrigerate for 1 day. Strain through cheesecloth, refrigerate for 1 more day, and then decant.

## Herb Oil

Yield: 1 cup

*1/2 cup chives*
*1 cup flat-leaf parsley*
*1/2 cup watercress*
*1 1/3 cups grapeseed oil*
*2/3 cup olive oil*

METHOD  Blanch the herbs in boiling salted water for 15 seconds. Immediately shock in ice water and drain. Coarsely chop the herbs and squeeze out the excess water. Place in a blender with the oil and purée for 3 to 4 minutes, or until bright green. Pour into a container, cover, and refrigerate for 1 day. Strain through cheesecloth, refrigerate for 1 more day, and then decant.

## Tarragon Oil

Yield: 1 cup

*1 cup tarragon*
*3/4 cup grapeseed oil*
*1/4 cup olive oil*

METHOD  Blanch the tarragon in boiling salted water for 15 seconds. Immediately shock in ice water and drain. Squeeze out the excess water and coarsely chop. Place in a blender with the oil and purée for 3 to 4 minutes, or until bright green. Pour into a container, cover, and refrigerate for 1 day. Strain through a cheesecloth, refrigerate 1 more day, and then decant.

# Reductions and Stocks

## Beef Stock Reduction

Yield: 1 1/4 cups

*10 pounds beef bones*
*2 carrots, coarsely chopped*
*2 stalks celery, coarsely chopped*
*1 yellow onion, coarsely chopped*
*1 leek, cleaned and coarsely chopped*
*1 bulb garlic, cut in half*
*2 tablespoons grapeseed oil*
*1/2 cup tomato concassée*
*4 cups red wine*

METHOD  Place the bones in a roasting pan and roast in the oven at 450 degrees for 2 hours, or until golden brown. In a large stock pot, caramelize the carrots, celery, onion, leeks, and garlic in the grapeseed oil. Add the tomato concassée and cook for 5 minutes. Deglaze with the red wine and reduce until most of the wine has been cooked out. Add the browned bones and cover with cold water. Bring to a boil, then reduce heat and let simmer over medium heat for 8 hours, skimming away the impurities that rise to the surface. Strain through a fine-mesh sieve and reduce over medium heat until it coats the back of a spoon.

## Blond Vegetable Stock

Yield: about 6 cups

*6 leeks, cleaned and coarsely chopped*
*4 Spanish onions, coarsely chopped*
*8 stalks celery, coarsely chopped*
*2 celery roots, peeled and coarsely chopped*
*2 turnips, peeled and coarsely chopped*
*2 parsnips, peeled and coarsely chopped*
*1 tablespoon whole black peppercorns*

METHOD  Place all of the vegetables and the peppercorns in a large stockpot. Cover with cold water and bring to a boil. Then reduce heat and simmer for 1 hour. Strain and reduce over medium heat to about 6 cups.

## Chicken Stock

Yield: about 6 cups

*15 pounds chicken bones*
*2 onions, coarsely chopped*
*2 carrots, coarsely chopped*
*4 stalks celery, coarsely chopped*
*1 bulb garlic, cut in half*
*1 bulb celery root, chopped*
*1 tablespoon whole black peppercorns*

METHOD  Place all of the ingredients in a large stockpot. Cover with cold water (about 2 gallons). Bring to a boil, reduce heat, and simmer over medium heat for 4 hours, skimming away impurities that rise to the surface. Strain and reduce over medium heat to about 6 cups.

## Red Wine Reduction

Yield: 1/2 cup

*1 onion, coarsely chopped*
*1 carrot, coarsely chopped*
*1 stalk celery, coarsely chopped*

*1 apple, coarsely chopped*
*2 cloves garlic*
*2 tablespoons grapeseed oil*
*2 bottles Burgundy*
*1 bottle Port wine*
*1 cup Chicken Stock (see above)*

METHOD  In a medium saucepan, caramelize the onion, carrot, celery, apple, and garlic in the grapeseed oil. Add the wine and reduce over medium heat for 2 hours. Strain and place in a small saucepan with the Chicken Stock. Continue to reduce over medium heat for 1 hour, or until you have 1/2 cup.

## Roasted Vegetable Stock

Yield: 6 cups

*2 carrots, peeled and coarsely chopped*
*2 Spanish onions, peeled and coarsely chopped*
*1 bulb celery root, peeled and coarsely chopped*
*2 red bell peppers, seeded and coarsely chopped*
*1 bulb fennel, cleaned and coarsely chopped*
*2 turnips, peeled and coarsely chopped*
*2 bulbs garlic, cut in half*
*2 tablespoons grapeseed oil*
*1 tablespoon whole black peppercorns*

METHOD  Place all of the vegetables and garlic on a sheet pan with 2 tablespoons grapeseed oil. Roast in the oven at 400 degrees for 40 minutes, or until golden brown. Remove from the oven, place in a large stockpot with the peppercorns, and cover with cold water. Bring to a boil, then simmer over medium heat for 1 hour. Strain, return to heat, and slowly reduce to 6 cups.

## Veal Stock Reduction

Yield: 1 1/4 cups

*10 pounds veal bones*
*2 carrots, coarsely chopped*
*2 stalks celery, coarsely chopped*
*1 yellow onion, coarsely chopped*
*1 leek, cleaned and coarsely chopped*
*1 bulb garlic, cut in half*
*2 tablespoons grapeseed oil*
*1/2 cup tomato concassée*
*4 cups red wine*

METHOD Place the bones in a roasting pan and roast in the oven at 450 degrees for 2 hours, or until golden brown. In a large stockpot, carmelize the carrots, celery, onion, leeks, and garlic in the grapeseed oil. Add the tomato concassée and cook for 5 minutes. Deglaze with the red wine and reduce until most of the wine has been cooked out. Add the browned bones and cover with cold water. Bring to a boil, then reduce heat and let simmer over medium heat for 8 hours. Strain through a fine-mesh sieve and reduce over medium heat until it coats the back of a spoon.

## Vegetable Stock

Yield: about 6 cups

*2 leeks, cleaned and coarsely chopped*
*4 Spanish onions, coarsely chopped*
*6 stalks celery, coarsely chopped*
*1 celery root, peeled and coarsely chopped*
*2 carrots, peeled and coarsely chopped*
*2 red bell peppers, seeded and coarsely chopped*
*1 rutabaga, peeled and coarsely chopped*
*1 fennel bulb, peeled and coarsely chopped*
*6 tomatoes, coarsely chopped*
*1 pound button mushrooms, cleaned*
*2 parsnips, peeled and coarsely chopped*
*2 bulbs garlic, cut in half*
*1 tablespoon whole black peppercorns*

METHOD Place all of the vegetables, the garlic, and the peppercorns in a large stockpot. Cover with cold water, bring to a boil, then reduce heat and simmer for 1 hour. Strain, return to heat, and slowly reduce to 6 cups.

Note: Vegetables may be omitted or substituted, depending on the flavor desired.

## Other Basics

### Anglaise Sauce

Yield: 1½ cups

*2 egg yolks*
*4 teaspoons sugar*
*1 cup heavy cream*

METHOD In a medium bowl, whisk together the yolks and sugar until smooth. Place the heavy cream in a small saucepan

and bring to a boil over medium heat. Temper the yolks with the hot cream while whipping constantly. Return the mixture to the saucepan. Cook over medium heat while stirring for 2 minutes, or until it coats the back of a spoon. Do not boil the mixture (because the eggs will curdle). Strain through a fine-mesh sieve and cool.

### Apple Chips

Yield: 12 chips

*12 paper-thin, crescent-shaped apple slices*

METHOD Lay the apple slices on a nonstick sheet pan and place in the oven at 225 degrees for 1 hour, or until lightly golden. Remove from the pan and store in an airtight container.

### Curry Butter

Yield: about ½ cup

*¼ cup chopped apple*
*1 clove garlic, chopped*
*1 shallot, chopped*
*1 teaspoon grapeseed oil*
*2 teaspoons curry powder*
*½ teaspoon paprika*
*2 tablespoons water*
*¼ cup butter, softened*

METHOD In a small saucepan, sauté the apple, garlic, and shallot in the grapeseed oil. Cook for 5 to 7 minutes over medium heat, then add the curry powder, paprika, and water. Continue to cook for 3 more minutes. Cool and fold in the soft butter. Purée with a small food processor or hand blender for 1 to 2 minutes until smooth. Pass through a fine-mesh sieve, cover, and refrigerate until needed.

### Oven-Dried Tomatoes

Yield: about 2 cups

*6 Roma tomatoes, cut in ¼-inch-thick slices*
*3 tablespoons olive oil*
*Salt and pepper*
*4 sprigs thyme*

METHOD Lay the sliced tomatoes on a wire rack and drizzle with olive oil. Season with salt and pepper and place the thyme on top of the tomatoes. Place in the oven at 275 degrees for 3 hours, or until slightly firm

and dry to the touch. Remove from the rack and refrigerate until needed. May be stored in the refrigerator for up to 3 days.

### Pâté Brisée

Yield: about 1 pound

*1¼ cups flour*
*2 tablespoons sugar*
*¾ teaspoon salt*
*⅔ cup cold butter, cubed*
*1 egg yolk*
*3 tablespoons ice water*

METHOD Place the flour, sugar, salt, and butter in a mixing bowl. Using the paddle attachment, mix on low until all the ingredients are combined and the texture is coarse. Add the yolk and water all at once, and mix on low until it just starts to come together. Remove the dough from the mixer and work into a ball on a floured surface. Wrap the dough in plastic and place in the refrigerator for 30 minutes, or until you are ready to use it.

### Preserved Ginger

Yield: 4 tablespoons

*6 tablespoons julienned gingerroot*
*1½ cups sugar*
*1½ cups water*

METHOD In a small saucepan place the ginger, ½ cup of the sugar, and ½ cup of the water. Bring to a simmer for 10 minutes. Strain the liquid and repeat the process two more times, reserving the final cooking liquid to store the ginger. Keep in the refrigerator until needed.

### Roasted Bell Peppers

Yield: about 1½ cups

*4 bell peppers*
*3 tablespoons olive oil*

METHOD Coat the whole bell peppers with olive oil. Place on an open grill or flame and roast until black on one side, about 3 minutes. Turn, and repeat. Place the roasted peppers in a bowl, cover with plastic wrap, and let stand for 5 minutes. Peel off the skin. Seed, remove the stems, and cut the peppers to the desired size.

## Roasted Garlic Purée

Yield: about ¾ cup

*4 bulbs garlic, tops cut off*
*3 cups milk*
*½ cup olive oil*
*Salt and pepper*

METHOD Place the garlic in a small saucepan, cover with the milk, and simmer for 10 minutes. Drain the milk, place the garlic bulbs bottom side down in an oven-proof pan, add the olive oil, and cover. Bake at 350 degrees for 1 to 1½ hours, or until the bulbs are soft. Once cool, squeeze the soft garlic out of the skins and place in a blender with the olive oil it baked in. Purée until smooth and season to taste with salt and pepper. If you prefer a thinner purée, you may adjust the consistency with Chicken Stock (page 229) or water.

## Roasted Mushrooms

Yield: about 2 cups

*3 cups wild mushrooms, cleaned*
*½ cup chopped Spanish onion*
*1 clove garlic*
*1 sprig thyme or rosemary*
*2 tablespoons olive oil*
*¾ cup Mushroom Juice (page 228) or water*
*Salt and pepper*

METHOD Place the mushrooms in an oven-proof pan and toss with the onion, garlic, thyme, and olive oil. Add the stock or water and season with salt and pepper. Cover and bake in the oven at 325 degrees for 30 to 40 minutes, or until the mushrooms are tender. Remove from the oven and let cool in the cooking juices.

## Semolina Pasta

Yield: ¾ pound

*2 cups extra-fine semolina flour*
*3 eggs*

METHOD Place the semolina flour and eggs in a mixing bowl. Using the dough hook, blend on low for 3 minutes, or until it comes together. Form into a ball, cover with plastic wrap, and refrigerate for 30 to 60 minutes before using.

## Tomato Water

Yield: 4 cups

*12 large beefsteak tomatoes*
*1 tablespoon salt*

METHOD Blend the tomatoes and salt in a food processor. Tie up the contents in cheesecloth and allow the liquid to drip into a large bowl. It is best to do this overnight in the refrigerator. The color of the Tomato Water will vary with the type of the tomato used and the time of year. Tomato Water can be kept for 3 to 4 days in the refrigerator, or it can be frozen.

# Cooking Terms, Equipment, Ingredients, and Techniques

BALSAMIC VINEGAR (*aceto balsamico*) A dark, sweet, mellow wine vinegar that is aged in a series of oak and hickory barrels. It is produced only in Modena, Italy. Used primarily as a dressing. The older the vinegar, the sweeter and less acidic it is.

BATON (*bâtonnet*) A cut the size of a wooden matchstick (⅛ by ⅛ by 2 inches).

BLACK CORINTH GRAPES Very tiny delicate purple-red grape clusters. These sweet grapes have no seeds and thin skins. They are temperature sensitive and must be kept cool once picked.

BLACK CURRANTS A tiny berry related to the gooseberry. They are often used for preserves or syrups, but they are also good to eat fresh.

BLACK GARBANZO BEANS A black version of garbanzo beans, which are also known as chickpeas. They are slightly larger than the average pea. They have a firm texture and mild nutlike flavor. They are used extensively in the Mediterranean, India, and Middle East.

BLACK JAPONICA RICE Small rice grains that are either dark black or deep red in color depending on the crop. The rice has a rich nutty flavor and is often used in Thai recipes.

BLANCHING AND SHOCKING To plunge a food into boiling salted water briefly and then to immediately place into ice water to stop the cooking process. Often used to firm the flesh or loosen the skins of fruits such as peaches or tomatoes. Also used to heighten and set color and flavor of herbs and greens.

BONIATO A white sweet potato that is a staple in Vietnam and Mexico.

BRUNOISE A very fine dice, approximately ⅛ square inch.

BURDOCK A slender root vegetable with a rusty brown skin and grayish white flesh. Cultivated primarily in Japan, it grows wild throughout Europe and the United States. It has a sweet, earthy flavor and a tender-crisp texture.

CALYPSO BEANS A dried legume that is white and black speckled.

CARDOON Resembles a giant bunch of wide, flat celery. It tastes like a cross between artichoke, celery, and salsify.

CATTAILS This wild shoot grows in woodland areas in the United States and Canada. It is found in muddy-water parts of woodlands. Most-used section is the midsection of the cattail. It is best to use underdeveloped cattails because they tend to be more savory.

CAULIFLOWER MUSHROOMS An off-white wild mushroom that resembles a head of cauliflower in appearance but not in flavor. It is tender with a mild mushroom essence.

CELLOPHANE NOODLES (bean threads, vermicelli) Clear noodles made from mung beans and sold in dry form. To cook, drop in boiling water for 1 minute. Available in Asian markets.

CHESTNUT HONEY A honey with a dark amber color and a unique and pungent scent. It is sweet with an interesting bittersweet aftertaste.

CHIFFONADE Fine strips, about 1/16 inch wide. Usually used in reference to leafy vegetables, which are rolled up and finely sliced.

CRÈME FRAÎCHE A true crème fraîche is a unpasteurized 30-percent cream that has been allowed to ferment and thicken naturally. It has a nutty, faintly sour flavor. In the United States, crème fraîche is made with whipping cream and buttermilk. Do not substitute sour cream.

DANDELION GREENS A weed that grows both wild and cultivated. The greens have jagged-edge leaves which have a slightly bitter, tangy flavor.

DEGLAZE When foods have been sautéed or roasted, the coagulated juices collect in the pan. Deglazing is the process of adding liquid to the pan and dissolving these flavorful deposits over heat.

DRAGON'S TONGUE BEANS Flat light yellow beans with purple specks about 3 to 4 inches long. The purple specks dissappear when cooked.

ENNIS HAZELNUTS Organic hazelnuts from the Trufflebert Farm in Oregon.

FILO/WHOLE WHEAT FILO Tissue-thin layers of pastry dough used in various Greek and Near East sweet and savory preparations. It is packaged fresh and frozen.

GELATIN Sheet gelatin is commonly used in Europe; here you may find it at some specialty food shops. If unavailable, substitute 1 teaspoon of gelatin granules for each leaf of sheet gelatin.

GLASSWORT Known as sea beans, or samphire as well. It grows along both the Pacific and Atlantic coasts. It has spiky green leaves that are arranged so that the plants look somewhat like a miniature cactus. Both the leaves and stems are crisp and taste of the sea.

GLUCOSE The most common form of this sugar is dextroglucose. It is also called corn sugar or grape sugar. It has about half the sweetening power of regular sugar. Because it doesn't crystallize easily, it is ideal for ice creams and sorbets.

HAWAIIAN GINGER A tamer, slightly more exotic-flavored ginger. It is not as harsh as regular ginger.

HOISIN A thick, sweet, brownish red sauce made with soybeans, vinegar, sesame seeds, chiles, and garlic. Used in Chinese cooking.

IRISH COBBLER POTATO A small creamy potato with a thin light brown skin and a soft yellow interior.

JUICING Extracting the juice from fruits or vegetables. Electric kitchen juicers are most effective.

KASHI A mixture of seven different grains including coarsely cut whole oats, long-grain barley, rye, hard red winter wheatberries, triticale, raw buckwheat barley, and hulled sesame seeds.

LAMB'S QUARTERS GREENS A small flat-leaf green which has defined points and a fuzz similar to a peach on both sides.

LEMONGRASS A scented grass used as an herb in Southeast Asian cooking. Although the whole stalk may be used, usually the outer leaves are removed and only the bottom third of the stalk is used. Has a lemony strawlike flavor.

LIPSTICK PEPPERS Small 2-inch-long red peppers, which are slightly pointy and have a thick flesh.

LOBSTER MUSHROOMS Wild mushrooms which are quite large with a bright red-orange flesh. The mushroom mimics the tender and chewy texture of lobster meat and the color of its shell.

LOLLA ROSSA GREENS A frilly deep red lettuce which grows in small heads and has a sweet delicate flavor.

LOQUAT (Japanese plum) The loquat resembles an apricot in size and color. The juicy, crisp flesh is pale yellow and has a delicate, sweetly tart flavor. It is available in Asian markets.

LOVAGE A member of the celery family, with dark green leaves that resemble celery or flat-leaf parsley. An easily grown perennial. The leaves are variously described as tasting of celery, lemon, yeast, pine, and/or basil.

MIRLITON (chayote) This gourdlike fruit is about the size of a very large pear. Beneath the pale green skin is a white, rather crisp flesh surrounding one soft seed. It is grown in several states including California, Florida, and Louisiana.

MISO A fermented soybean paste used in Japanese cooking for making soups, sauces, and dressings. Three types of miso are available at most supermarkets; red, yellow, and white. The three types are very distinct in flavor and should not be substituted for one another.

MITSUBA A small green herb or lettuce that resembles flat-leaf parsley. The leaves have a sharp pepper taste and the fragile stem has a somewhat stronger bite.

NAPE To just coat the back of a spoon.

NORI Paper-thin sheets of dried seaweed. The color can range from dark green to black. It is generally used for wrapping sushi. When finely cut, it serves as a seasoning or garnish.

OBLIQUE A vegetable cut that is neither perpendicular nor parallel to one end, creating a wedge with two straight sides and one following the natural curve of the vegetable.

PAVÉ Any layered preparation cut into a square or rectangle that resembles an old-fashioned paving stone (*pavé*).

POBLANO A dark green chile pepper that can vary from mild to hot. The darkest poblanos have the richest flavor. The best poblanos are found in Central Mexico.

PUMPKIN SEED OIL Also know as kernol. An oil made from the roasting and pressing of pumpkin seeds. It is produced in Styria.

QUENELLE An oval dumpling made with a forcemeat of fish, veal, or poultry. By extension, the term is also used to mean the typical oval shape. Quenelles can be easily formed with two spoons.

QUINCE A yellow-skinned fruit that looks and tastes like a cross between an apple and a pear. Its texture and flavor become enhanced when cooked. Select those that are large, firm, and yellow with little or no sign of green.

RAMP (wild leek) A wild onion that resembles a baby leek with broad leaves.

RICE BEANS Small white beans that are slightly larger than a cooked piece of rice when dry. They have a delicate skin and sweet flavor.

ROSEMARY SKEWERS Long thick stems of rosemary with a 1- or 2-inch portion of the herb at the top of the stem. They are used the same as a bamboo skewer.

SALSIFY A root vegetable imported from Belgium. It is available in specialty produce markets. When peeled, the flesh will discolor unless immediately placed in milk or acidulated water.

SAPOTE (white sapote) This fruit has a pale, creamy flesh that is usually soft and juicy. It has a very sweet, mild flavor that may hint of peaches, lemons, mango, and coconut.

SHISO (perilla, beefsteak plant) A member of the mint family. Somewhat tangy; tastes like a cross between lemon and mint. Often used as a garnish in Japanese cooking.

SUNCHOKE (Jerusalem artichoke) This vegetable is not truly an artichoke; it is a variety of sunflower with a lumpy, brown-skinned tuber that resembles gingerroot. The white flesh is nutty, sweet, and crisp.

SWEAT To cook, uncovered, slowly, over medium or low heat with very little fat, until soft or translucent.

TAMARI A dark soy sauce, somewhat thicker and stronger than other soy sauces. It is cultured and fermented like miso. Used in Asian cooking; in Japanese cuisine, it is used as a dipping or basting sauce.

TAMARIND The fruit of a tall shade tree native to Asia. The large 5-inch-long pods contain small seeds and a sour-sweet pulp, which when dried becomes extremely sour.

TANGO GREENS A frilly bright green lettuce with a delicate flavor.

TATSOI A round small leaf green with a mild flavor.

TEMPER To slowly add a hot liquid to a cold substance while constantly whisking until the cold liquid is warm. This is often done in ice cream and custard preparations to prevent the egg yolks from curdling.

TERRINE A mold, usually rectangular in shape. Also, the food, which is usually layered, that has been prepared in the terrine.

For recipes in this book, the terrine need not be ovenproof. If you have a terrine that is too large for a given recipe, you can reduce its capacity by filling the extra space with pieces of raw potato. Line the area to be used with plastic wrap or aluminum foil and proceed with the recipe.

TIMBALE A mold generally high-sided, drum-shaped and slightly tapered at one end. It is often used to bake custard.

TOGARASHI An Asian spice made of dried chiles, black sesame seeds, and dried herbs.

TOMATILLO A small, hard, round green fruit that looks and tastes somewhat like a green tomato. Often sold with its peppery brown husk still on. Used extensively in Mexican and Southwestern cooking.

TOMATO CONCASSÉE Peeled, seeded, and diced tomato.

TOURNE A 1- to 2-inch-football-shaped cut of a vegetable with seven flat sides.

TREVISO A red-leafed Italian chicory, similar to the variety radicchio except the leaves are narrow and pointed. It has a slightly bitter flavor.

TROUT BEANS A dried legume which is red and deep burgundy speckled.

TRUFFLES A subterranean fungus that is highly prized for its pungent aroma and flavor; found only in certain regions of France and Italy. If fresh truffles are not available, substitute frozen truffles. Scrub thoroughly before using. White truffles are rarer and more expensive than black. Olive oils that have been infused with the highly pungent white truffle are available in gourmet shops.

TUILE A round wafer that is molded around a curved surface immediately as it comes out of the oven so that it resembles a curved tile (*tuile* in French).

WATER BATH A container filled with ice water that is used to quickly cool a food product (such as a stock or sauce.) A second, smaller container is placed in the water bath, allowing the food product to cool without directly touching the water bath. Also used to evenly cook delicate items (such as custards).

WATER CHESTNUTS Fresh water chestnuts are so far superior to the canned that you should accept no substitute. Boil for 10 minutes and peel before using. Available in most Asian markets.

WHEAT GRASS A 4-inch-long lawn grass rich in beta carotene and chlorophyll. It is often used in vegetable juice drinks.

WHITE and RED FRAISES DES BOIS Intensely sweet, tiny wild strawberries from France. They are very delicate and bruise easily.

WHITE ROSE POTATOES Sweet, creamy small potatoes with a thin, light brown skin and delicate flesh.

# Sources

Though it may take a little searching, you can probably find all of the ingredients you need right in your own area. For items that are not stocked by your supermarket, check out local ethnic markets and specialty food stores. If that fails, you can contact the suppliers listed below.

Charlie Trotter's
816 West Armitage
Chicago, Illinois 60614
(773) 248-6228
*The 8 by 1 1/2 by 2 1/4-inch terrine that was used in* Charlie Trotter's *and* Charlie Trotter's Vegetables *may be purchased through the restaurant.*

Dean and Deluca
560 Broadway
New York, New York 10012
(800) 221-7714
*White truffle oil, olive paste, balsamic vinegar, grains, beans, and more.*

Star Market
3349 North Clark Street
Chicago, Illinois 60657
(773) 472-0599
*Asian dry goods and produce.*

Geo. Cornille & Sons Produce
60 South Water Market
Chicago, Illinois 60608
(312) 226-1015
*Fresh produce and specialty produce.*

# Index

© 1996 by Charlie Trotter
Photographs © 1996 by Tim Turner

Ten Speed Press
P.O. Box 7123
Berkeley, California 94707
www.tenspeed.com

Distributed in Australia by Simon and Schuster Australia,
in Canada by Ten Speed Press Canada,
in New Zealand by Southern Publishers Group,
in South Africa by Real Rooks, and
in the United Kingdom and Europe by Airlift Book Company.


Project Coordinator and General Editor: Judi Carle, Charlie Trotter's
Editor: Lorena Jones, Ten Speed Press
Research, development and supplementary recipe testing:
Sari Zernich, Charlie Trotter's
Recipe testing: Susie Heller, Cleveland


Typeset in Monotype Walbaum by Paul Baker Typography, Inc., Chicago


Library of Congress Cataloging-in-Publication Data


Trotter, Charlie.
Charlie Trotter's vegetable / Charlie Trotter.
p.    cm.
Includes index.
ISBN 0-89815-838-9


1. Cookery (Vegetables)  2. Charlie Trotter's (Restaurant)
I. Title.
TX 801.T74 1996
641.6'5--dc20                96-3946
CIP


Printed in China by C & C Offset Printing Co., LTD.



4  5  6  7  8  9  10  —  08  07  06  05  04